Penguin Crossword Puzzles
Series Editor: Alan Cash

The Ninth Penguin Book
of *Sunday Times* Crosswords

Other *Sunday Times* Crossword Books in Penguin

Sunday Times Crosswords
The Second Penguin Book of Sunday Times Crosswords
The Third Penguin Book of Sunday Times Crosswords
The Fourth Penguin Book of Sunday Times Crosswords
The Fifth Penguin Book of Sunday Times Crosswords
The Sixth Penguin Book of Sunday Times Crosswords
The Seventh Penguin Book of Sunday Times Crosswords
The Eighth Penguin Book of Sunday Times Crosswords

The Ninth Penguin Book of *Sunday Times* Crosswords

Compiled by Barbara Hall
with Solver's Guide by Elizabeth and Derek Jewell

Penguin Books

PENGUIN BOOKS

Published by the Penguin Group
27 Wrights Lane, London W8 5TZ, England
Viking Penguin Inc., 40 West 23rd Street, New York, New York 10010, USA
Penguin Books Australia Ltd, Ringwood, Victoria, Australia
Penguin Books Canada Ltd, 2801 John Street, Markham, Ontario, Canada L3R 1B4
Penguin Books (NZ) Ltd, 182–190 Wairau Road, Auckland 10, New Zealand

Penguin Books Ltd, Registered Offices: Harmondsworth, Middlesex, England

First published in book form 1988
10 9 8 7 6 5 4 3 2 1

Filmset in Linotron Times by
Rowland Phototypesetting Ltd, Bury St Edmunds, Suffolk
Made and printed in Great Britain by
Cox and Wyman Ltd, Reading, Berks.

The Solver's Guide

1 Seventy Years of Crosswords

There are crazes and crazes. For a few brief months (occasionally, years) people wiggle in hula-hoops, loop the loop with yo-yos, enter marathon dance contests, bounce about on pogo sticks. The vogue hits a peak, then fades.

Well over half a century ago, it was thought that the crossword would be simply a craze, too. It was not. It has flourished, grown into all kinds of exotic forms, and arguably become the most enduring armchair game (if game it can be called) of our century. Its combination of mental stimulation, agony, entertainment and challenge is unique.

Crosswords are tradition. Crosswords are respectable. Crosswords have been called the opiate of the eggheads. Some crosswords, the very tantalizing and intellectual ones, may be. But they are surely more than that. Heaven knows precisely how many millions of human beings around the world attempt to solve a crossword every day. There is, however, some evidence about that. During the 1960s, a Gallup poll showed that crossword solvers in the USA numbered upwards of 30 million adults, beating bridge, bingo, chess, poker and checkers as that nation's most popular leisure-time activity. Of the thousands of daily and weekly newspapers in Britain and the USA, it's unlikely that more than one per cent go to press without a crossword. On the rare occasions that publications have tried to leave out their puzzles, howls of rage have arisen from their readers. During the Second World War, British newspapers were cut back to a mere four pages – but the crosswords stayed.

Is there, indeed, a more striking example of an Anglo-American 'special relationship' than the crossword puzzle? The first one appeared on Sunday 21 December 1913 in the old New York *World* (they called it a Word-Cross Puzzle), but the man who composed it, Arthur Wynne, was born in Liverpool, England. The idea didn't reach England till eleven years later, since when the two countries have vied to make bigger, better and more idiosyncratic puzzles.

It isn't, however, an Anglo-American monopoly. In Italy in 1955 there was a plea by one Dr Michele Quitadamo for crosswords to be made part of the school curriculum. 'Crosswords', he said, 'are a valuable form of gymnastics for the intelligence.' In October 1944 Paris newspapers stopped publishing crosswords for a time for fear they might be used to convey information to the Germans. In 1966, a lady in Fiji wrote to *The Times* to say she had just completed the puzzle published in the paper on 4 April 1932: her mother had begun it and she, finding the issue years later, had finished off the job. A Serbo-Croat crossword, with 40,000 squares and 8,469 clues (compiled by one Zvonko Janah), is claimed to be the biggest ever created, although there's rather firmer evidence about the effort of Mr Robert Stilgenbauer of Los Angeles, whose 3,185-clues-across – 3,149-clues-down puzzle took him years of spare time before publication in 1949. Despite the 125,000 copies distributed, no all-correct solution has been returned! The British educational weekly, *The Teacher*, received a congratulatory letter in 1971 from the Zambian High Commission. 'Several of us have been trying to fill in these crosswords ourselves,' it reads, 'but are not of sufficient calibre to finish them – yet.'

Still, it's in the English-speaking (or, should one say, English-and-American-speaking) world that the anecdotes grow thickest. Addiction to crosswords has been compared with eating peanuts, black coffee, opium, the detective story and self-flagellation. We like the story about Mr Ronald Knox who always gave up doing the *Times* daily crossword during Lent, as a penance. This particular crossword has been mentioned in plays, books and movies. (Very true. We were rewatching that old Noël Coward weepie *Brief Encounter* on TV one night, and there was Celia Johnson's boring but steadfast old husband doing his *Times* crossword and asking her to help him with it whilst she was sitting there dreaming only of her lover, Trevor Howard. Is that unfair to crossword addicts?) It's been quoted in the law courts as a standard against which the intelligence of witnesses has been judged. A puzzle a day has been prescribed by at least one doctor – and headshrinkers are always getting in on the act. A New York psychologist believes crosswords are popular because they are 'orderly', in contrast to the disorderly world facing the crossword buff beyond. 'Here is one problem he *can* solve himself.' People work out crosswords, says a psychiatrist, for the same reason children dismantle dolls or clockwork toys, or men explore space; they want to discover what goes on, to satisfy the universal urge of mankind to solve the unknown. A man was once charged and fined at a magistrates' court in Britain for cutting *Times* crosswords out of issues in a public library.

Mr Wynne, we're sure, didn't guess what he was starting back in 1913. One gathers that even he wasn't especially impressed with his effort, shoved in as a filler, which was a diamond-shaped block consisting of 72 white squares around a centre of black squares. He gave readers 32 interlocking words to be guessed and the clues were straight synonyms or definitions: 'Close of day' = evening, 'Day-dream' = reverie, and so on.

The game hadn't arrived out of thin air. Wynne was working a variation on this kind of word puzzle:

P H A S E
H O V E L
A V O I D
S E I N E
E L D E R

And that had been around virtually since the birth of Christ, developing into the acrostic puzzle which gave (as Wynne did) definitions for the words. Wynne's minor revolution was the idea that the words across could be different from the words going down.

Oddly enough, considering what finally happened to the crossword, there wasn't much reaction for almost a decade. One New York *World* editor recalled: 'The puzzle obviously had a big following, but was regarded in the office as beneath a sensible man's consideration.' Maybe the First World War and its gloomy aftermath took people's minds off anything as frivolous as word puzzles. Maybe the early crosswords were too full of typographers' errors for many solvers to get the idea. Indeed, as late as 1923 *The Times* appeared not even to have heard of the latest form of word puzzle since it felt it worth while to devote an editorial called 'The Tyranny of the Acrostic' to the crossword's precursor.

> The 'shop' of Acrostics is today becoming a form of conversation in which all can join. It is heard on every side . . . There are also some who may be called acrostic touts. They do not compete themselves but ply the lexicon on behalf of someone else, usually a lady, who has

several such guessing cavaliers in her train . . . More often than not they are left protesting that the composer has cheated them by some low device, some meaning of a word perhaps only to be found in an American dictionary.

In 1924, however, the crossword really came into its own. In Britain, the first newspaper crossword was published in the *Sunday Express*, while in America two bright young publishers named Richard Simon and Max Shuster brought out the first book of crosswords. Within a year it sold 400,000 copies at $1.35 under the imprint of the Plaza Publishing Company (because Messrs S. and S. were ashamed, at first, for it to be known as *their* book?) and, with sales of dictionaries and *Roget's Thesaurus* also rocketing, the fad was established.

Most newspapers began to publish daily crosswords. In America there were crossword tournaments galore – Yale against Harvard, Brooklyn against Manhattan, cops versus firemen – while a Chicago wife was given a divorce on the grounds that she had become a 'crossword widow'. In London, pickpockets were reportedly doing good business either by helping solvers in hotel lobbies or by pretending to be solvers themselves and seeking the assistance of prospective victims. And the New York *World*, which had started it all, got a poet (Gelett Burgess) to compile a crossword for them, announcing it aptly:

> The fans they chew their pencils,
> The fans they beat their wives,
> They look up words for extinct birds –
> They live such puzzling lives.

Yet the crossword, hailed in America as 'the greatest known foe of boredom', was to become rather a bore itself once the composers began to run out of obvious words. During the mid-1920s, crosswords became bogged down with a sticky mass of exotic and unfamiliar words, so much so that in America the *Bookman* magazine could publish a long dialogue between two women which went in part like this:

MRS W.: What is that you're working at, my dear?
MRS F.: I'm tatting Joe's initials on his moreen vest. Are you making that ebon garment for yourself?
MRS W.: Yea. Just a black dress for everyday. Henry says I look rather naïf in black.

MRS F.: Well, perhaps; but it's a bit too anile for me. Give me something in indigo, or, say, ecru.
MRS W.: Quite right. There is really no neb in such solemn vestments.
MRS F.: Stet.
MRS W.: By the way, didn't I hear that your little Junior met with an accident?
MRS F.: Yes. The little oaf fell from an apse and fractured his artus.
MRS W.: Egad!

Not, in truth, that the fashion for such cliché crossword phrases has ever died out entirely. In 1959, under the heading 'Crossword Country', the letters page of *The Times* had a running correspondence about the subject. A reader in Paris wrote:

> Sir – I have amused myself recently by visualising 'Crossword Country'. It consists largely of tors covered with heather (ling) and the predominating fauna are ernes, hens, lions, asps and she-cats. They feed, as appropriate, on grubs, sole, bass, ants, bees and each other. There are, unfortunately, also humans, all dastards, renegades or rips, except for some dons, doctors, Royal Engineers and tars (A.B.s). Their names are Mac, Ian, or Eli. This regrettable population is kept going with the collaboration of lasses or maids named Eve and Vera who, necessarily, become Ma, as Mac and Co. become Pa.

To which another correspondent, among many, added:

> Three birds should, I think, be added to the fauna: the emu, dodo and kiwi. Mammals very much in evidence include agouta, agouti, coati, koala, okapi and panda. As for humans, there is a handsome gaggle of girls: Mimi, Fifi, Gigi, Bebe, Hebe, Hera, Hero and Dido. Their boyfriends cannot all be enumerated. Some have names of Biblical provenance: Elihu, Agag, Noah, and his sons. Beeri and Sisera. Others frequently encountered include Plato, Cato, Tito, Omar, Odo, Koko, Casca, Cicero. Bob and Penny (referred to by their initials) become increasingly active: should Bob ail, we are about to leave port; but should Penny ail, we are legislating for Eire.*

It was clear that the crossword had to get out of the rut of rocs, emus, apods and apses into which it had slipped. And, jointly, it was probably the *New York Times* and *The Times* of London which did the most to widen the scope of the puzzle.

* 'Bob ail' = S ('s' was the abbreviation for 'shilling' or 'bob') + AIL = SAIL (about to leave port). 'Penny ail' = D (former abbreviation for 'penny') + AIL = DAIL (Irish legislative assembly).

The New York paper was the leader with innovations such as phrases instead of single words in the grids, quotations with missing words, and the use of proper names and topical references. 'Having your name appear in the Sunday crossword is like getting free room and board in the Hall of Fame for a week,' a celebrity once observed. And once *The Times* added its thunder, the pace quickened still more.

The first daily crossword appeared in *The Times* on 1 February 1930, in response to a suggestion in a letter from one Lieutenant-Commander A. C. Powell. It had a rough ride early on – 'pandering to the modern craze for passing the time in all sorts of stupid ways', one correspondent among scores of angry readers bewailed – and it took a veteran American solver over an hour and a half to finish. So livid were the complaints that Auntie *Times* was compromising her dignity, that crosswords in Latin and Greek were swiftly published in an attempt to gain respectability. Then came the development of ever more involved puzzles with anagrams, sometimes avowed, sometimes cunningly disguised; ghastly puns; inversions; subtle divisions of words and phrases to suggest meanings different from their surface interpretation; bizarre allusions to history, geography, literature, music, sports and games. The crossword audience of *The Times* was seen as an 'eclectic, versatile, whimsical, cultivated fellowship – an audience of intellectual magpies', grappling with the compiler in 'an ever-renewed but always good-tempered battle of wits, in which the last thing that anyone wants is a final victory for either side'. The compiler himself was imagined to be 'a canon of Barchester and a member of the Pickwick Club [who] attends concerts of classical music only but keeps in touch with the frivolities of the contemporary stage, regrets the advance of mechanisation but consoles himself by growing rare blooms for the Royal Horticultural Society's shows'. He was actually several people, but most notably Mr Adrian Bell, who composed Crossword No. 1, wore out a dictionary a year, and whose fiancée was congratulated by her prospective father-in-law thus: 'You have the sort of mind which will help Adrian with his crosswords.'

In those early days there were constant outbreaks of letters to *The Times* from crossword fans, who included Ian Hay, Sir Max Beerbohm, John Masefield, P. G. Wodehouse and the

Archbishop of York. Among the most interesting was one (August 1934) which went:

> I want to claim a record. A few weeks ago, when no policeman was looking, a bookstall keeper in Berlin boldly sold me a copy of *The Times*. I started the crossword as the train left and finished it 40 hours later, when I arrived at Moscow. Can anyone beat this? Time must be taken off for such sleep as can be got on a train and a considerable time spent in convincing officials on the Russian frontier that I had no firearms concealed on my person. Sir Austen Chamberlain claims that the Provost of Eton polishes off these puzzles while his breakfast egg is boiling. If it boiled while he did this one, I say without hesitation that, while the school may have been Eton, I am quite sure the egg wasn't.

The crossword was, at the same time, being hailed as having made travel so much more interesting, revolutionised the life of the Stock Exchange and eliminated the silence barriers between permanent residents in hotels. By September 1938, when Chamberlain was heralding the false dawn of Munich, *The Times* could write an ingenuous editorial which began: 'Who would have thought 15 years ago that the crossword puzzle had come to stay? To most of us then it looked like a transatlantic craze which could not be expected to take root in solid, unimaginative British minds.' Later, in May 1944, before the Anglo-American invasion of northern Europe had taken place, *The Times* was still at it. 'The sight of our fellow travellers in a suburban railway carriage, each with contracted brow and tapping pencil attacking his daily crossword, makes us wonder whether as a race we are growing more intellectual.'

We don't really swallow that, but certainly the development of crosswords since the Second World War has tended increasingly to make the clues themselves more baffling rather than the answers. Obscure words as answers seem to us to be the desperate last resort of a composer. In over thirty years of puzzle compiling, the last twenty for the *Sunday Times* (which has run puzzles since the 1920s), we have not always been above doing that ourselves, but we regard the need to put in bizarre answers as a defeat. The compiler's job, we think, should be to wrap up reasonably ordinary words in clues which are ultimately seen to be fair by the solver, but which, until the moment of breakthrough, disguise the answer in the wittiest possible way. Word play is the summit of crossword achievement and clues should encourage the imagination of the solver to expand, to freewheel through all kinds of word-and-idea associations. The sort of clues we most enjoy are the cryptics. Such clues have a huge range, which we shall be explaining later, but a few examples will give the idea. The answer to the clue 'Rough's companion' is 'Ready'; 'Evergreen creeper' leads to 'Grass snake' (isn't that beautifully succinct and precise?); and 'It is topping to kiss a monkey' works out as 'Apex' ('Ape' + 'X').

British puzzles at their best tend to be the most avant-garde in the world. Yet even the most daunting clues should be understandable once the ground rules of the game are known – even that clue from *The Times* which read 'Anne of Cleves cried "No"!', to which the answer was 'Neighed'. The solver here is required to have cognisance of the fact that Anne of Cleves was known as the 'Flanders Mare'! When *The Times* holds its regular National Crossword Contest it does indeed strain the quick-wittedness and breadth of knowledge of those who enter. Many thousands of readers enter this competition each year. In 1970, for example, there were 20,000 entrants and, of the 2,000 who were left by the time of the final elimination puzzle, half were knocked out by a clue which called for knowledge of the word 'uffish', which is contained in the invented vocabulary of Lewis Carroll's poem 'Jabberwocky', from *Through the Looking Glass* (the poem that begins ''Twas brillig, and the slithy toves did gyre and gimble in the wabe'). Most of them wrote 'uppish' as the answer. There was another clue which gave trouble. It read, 'They hang from trees in the Book of Jeremiah', to which the answer was 'Amenta' (catkins). Perhaps the compiler may almost sadistically have imagined frantic competitors scouring the Book of Jeremiah to find the answer, when there it was all the time, staring them in the face as a 'contained word' in the very title of the book, which correctly reads: 'the l**amenta**tions of Jeremiah'. It may be a humbling thought that the record time for completing the *Times* crossword under test conditions is 3 minutes 45 seconds by a civil servant named Roy Dean from Bromley, Kent, on 19 December 1970, in a BBC studio during the course of a programme called 'Today'!

We promise nothing as devilish as that 'Jeremiah' clue or 'uffish' in the puzzles in this book, but to solve them you need to know something about the conventions of cryptic crosswords. If you're already an experienced solver, you may (except out of curiosity) stop reading now. But if you're a (relative) newcomer, an explanation of the more important ground rules may help.

2 How to Solve Cryptic Crosswords

Word play is the essence of cryptic crosswords. It can appear in many forms in the clues, but the chief kinds are these:

a Word divisions
b Liberties with punctuation, etc.
c Inversions of words or parts of words; leaving out bits of words, etc.
d Anagrams
e 'Contained-word' or hidden clues
f 'Sound-word' clues
g Use of abbreviations
h Disguise of verbs as nouns, nouns as verbs, etc.
i Puns and double meanings
j Overt or disguised references to literature, etc.
k Special crossword conventions
l Quotations

We'll lead you through examples of each of these before arriving at a complete specimen of a cryptic crossword with an explanation of each answer. Some of the examples given – though by no means all – are taken from puzzles in this series.

a *Word divisions*
Many words given as answers in crosswords split into two or more words which have meaning in themselves. Take the word 'redstart', which is a kind of bird. It breaks into 'red' + 'start', and a simple cryptic clue for this could be 'Revolutionary innovation by a bird'. The clue indicates 'red' by the straight synonym 'revolutionary', and 'start' by another straight synonym, 'innovation'; it also indicates the meaning of the whole answer by telling you it's 'a bird'. This is the most straightforward way of clueing an answer on the principle of word division.

Sometimes words (e.g. 'added to', 'receiving', etc.) will be put into the clue indicating that parts of the answer 'join up' to form the whole. An example would be:

'The embassy *receives* a sign from heaven: must be religious types! (12)'

Answer: MISSIONARIES – in which MISSION is 'the embassy', plus ARIES as 'a sign from heaven', ending up as MISSIONARIES, who are 'religious types'.

An answer may also be broken up into two or more words, however, in a different way. Take the word 'defenders'. This can be broken up thus: DEF(END)ERS, i.e. the word END is included in the word DEFERS. A clue for this would, quite fairly, read: 'They don't attack delays without consequence (9)'. The answer DEFENDERS is defined by 'They don't attack'; DEFERS is defined by its synonym 'delays' (which misleads you in the clue because you should read it as a *verb*, but it looks as if it's a noun); and DEFERS is stated to be 'without' (i.e. 'outside', though, again, this isn't the obvious way to read it) the word END, given in the clue as its synonym 'consequence'.

This kind of word-division clue is frequently signalled by the use of certain give-away words in clues. Apart from the cunning 'without', other such phrases are 'outside', 'inside', 'among', 'holding', 'surrounding', 'interrupting'. Here are examples of these – and at this point we're going to start using a shorthand form of explanation which shows how the answers are broken up in the clue. The italicized words would not normally be italicized, but are here put in this form to emphasize the 'instruction' word(s) in the clues:

'French nobleman *among* the offspring led astray (7)'

Answer: SEDUCED – SE(DUC)ED.

'Attack the stupid creature who's *holding* one back (8)'

Answer: DENOUNCE – D(ENO)UNCE (NB 'one back' = 'one reversed').

'Was still adopting an assumed attitude in revolutionary *surroundings* (7)'

Answer: REPOSED – RE(POSE)D (NB 'reposed' means 'was still').

'Famous naturalist and doctor interrupted by a triumph (6)'

Answer: DARWIN – D(A)R/WIN (DR – 'doctor' – interrupted by 'A', plus WIN – 'triumph').

b *Liberties with punctuation, etc.*

You've already noticed, no doubt, that in some of the sample clues given above, part of the mystification is caused by omission of punctuation which, were it there, would help the solver a great deal to read the clue as it *should* be read in order to arrive at the answer. Had there been a full stop or semicolon or dash after 'Was still' it would have made the solving easier, but the fun less. You'll find many examples of liberties with punctuation in cryptic crosswords. It's part of the game. Never accept at face value the way a clue *appears* to read. Look at these samples:

'A heavyweight goes to Alabama for an unusual kind of music (6)'

Answer: ATONAL – A/TON/AL. We all know that a TON is a 'heavy weight'; but when the two words are run together, the image is of a boxer rather than anything else – and it's meant to mislead. AL is used as an abbreviation for 'Alabama'.

'Tom following Diana – indeed devoted! (9)'

Answer: DEDICATED – DE(DICAT)ED. A tricky clue, but one which reveals a very common crossword convention. 'Diana' is DI; she's followed by CAT ('Tom'); and the whole lot is '*in* DEED', but those two words have been run together to make 'indeed' with the intention of defying the solver. But you won't let compilers frustrate you for long if you remember that nine times out of ten (well, maybe eight), the word 'indeed' in a clue signifies that you're trying to wrap 'de—ed' around something else. (Cf. also the word 'inside', which often needs to be read 'in side'.)

c *Inversions of words or parts of words; leaving out bits of words, etc.*

Once you've discovered that answers can be broken up into separate parts, be prepared also for the way in which compilers will signal to you that those parts have got to be treated in particular ways. Here's an example:

'I'm reversing to run at top speed, or is that literally wrong? (8)'

Answer: MISPRINT – MI/SPRINT. The phrase 'I'm' in the clue is reversed to make 'MI'; 'to run at top speed' is a definition of SPRINT; and MISPRINT is defined (with a touch of pun) in the clue as something that's 'literally wrong'. So watch out in clues for words like 'overturned', 'upset', 'return', 'going back', 'set back', 'climbing' (in down clues) as well as 'reverse', all of which indicate that a part of the answer (or the whole answer) contains a part of the clue (or its synonym) *reversed*.

A still further variation of these tricks is that the clue will indicate that the answer contains only *part* of what the clue is giving you. A few examples are better than generalised explanations to give you the idea.

'Opening your mouth and losing your head in the shelter (6)'

Answer: AWNING – (Y)AWNING. 'Opening your mouth' would be 'yawning'. It loses its 'head' (i.e. its first letter) to become AWNING, a 'shelter'.

'He lost his head, then ran with long strides and escaped with the girl! (6)'

Answer: ELOPED – (H)E/LOPED. 'He lost his head' indicates the letter E; 'ran with long strides' defines LOPED; and 'escaped with the girl' indicates the answer, ELOPED.

'Speaking acidly, as it were, when giving can back to unvigorous Richard (6)'

Answer: NITRIC – NIT/RIC(HARD). 'Can back' in the clue indicates 'tin' reversed to give NIT; 'unvigorous Richard' means that the part of 'Richard' meaning 'vigorous' ('hard') is omitted to give RIC; 'Speaking acidly' points to the answer, NITRIC.

'Apportions great quantities to Alabama first (6)'

Answer: ALLOTS – AL/LOTS. 'Great quantities' in the clue signifies LOTS in the answer: 'Alabama' points to AL, an abbreviation for 'Alabama', and 'first' indicates that you've to put AL before LOTS; 'apportions' in the clue is the meaning of the whole answer, ALLOTS.

To indicate *all* the warning signs in clues which will tell you that bits of words or whole words are to be moved around would be impossible, but as soon as you see expressions like 'un-', 'headless', 'beheaded', 'doesn't start', 'doesn't begin', then beware. Note, too, that the phrases 'I leave' or 'I omitted' will often mean that the letter 'i' is going to be dropped out of a word (or synonym) in the clue in order to build up the answer (e.g., 'I leave the point with nothing on to reach part of the bridge' would give the answer PONTOON – PO(I)NT/O/ON) and that the word 'pointless' will similarly indicate that one of the letters 'N', 'W', 'E' or 'S' (the points of the compass) is going to be dropped out of the build-up given in the clue. One favourite convention is also worth a note. The clue 'Everyone in bed is hauled ashore' would obviously give the answer BEACHED – B(EACH)ED; but the compiler could easily take the clue a stage further and make it read, 'Everyone *between sheets* is hauled ashore' (which would be still more baffling since 'sheets' means 'ropes' on a boat).

d *Anagrams*

An anagram is a word or phrase formed by rearranging the letters of another word or phrase. In the old crossword days, anagrams were labelled clearly as such; so a clue might read simply, 'Caned (anag.)'. Answer: DANCE. But today, anagrams are indicated much more subtly. Any word in a clue which can possibly mean, either literally or figuratively, that the order of the letters in other words in the clue is to be changed may give you the tip that you've got an anagram on your hands. Let's start by giving you a few examples. In the simplest anagram one word (or several words in succession) is (are) the one(s) from which you're going to make up the answer. Like this:

'When *a male* is mangled no wonder you have a feeling of sickness! (7)'

> *Answer:* MALAISE. You've been told to 'mangle' ('mutilate') the phrase 'a male is' – rather appropriately in view of the answer.

The next stage of an anagram is when the words you're looking for are *not* consecutive, but are linked by other words – most simply by the link words 'and' or 'with', as in this clue:

'Bit of the plumbing that gives both *pride* and *pain* (9)'

> *Answer:* DRAINPIPE. Out of which you can get (or be 'given') the two words 'pride' and 'pain'.

Thirdly, a clue may be a *part* anagram, as in this one:

'Ride at medium pace and forget the *least* variety of Eng. Lit.! (10, 5)'

> *Answer:* CANTERBURY TALES – CANTER/BURY TALES. In this clue 'Ride at medium pace' = CANTER; 'forget' = BURY; whilst TALES is a 'variety' of 'least' in the clue.

Fourthly, anagrams may be accompanied by instructions to remove letters from the anagram words or to substitute other letters (a similar convention to that under heading c). Here are three examples:

'*A pound* perhaps with *a* substitute for *love* from Italy (6)'

Answer: PADUAN. The anagram words are 'a pound', indicated by 'perhaps' – but you've been instructed to substitute 'a' for 'o' ('O' = 'love' in tennis scoring), and if you do you'll find that 'a paund' will make PADUAN (someone 'from Italy').

'Disorder makes one *sell out* – and *left* out too! (6)'

Answer: TOUSLE. The word TOUSLE ('Disorder' in the clue) will 'make one' the words 'sell out', except that one 'l' must disappear, which is indicated by the phrase 'left out' ('l' being the recognised abbreviation for 'left').

'Pillar constructed to order with endlessly varied skill (7)'

Answer: OBELISK – O.B.E./LISK. Here, the answer is described by 'Pillar' in the clue; you 'construct' it by placing an 'order' (O.B.E., Officer of the Order of the British Empire) with 'endlessly varied skill', which signifies 'skil' ('skill' without its final 'l', i.e. 'endlessly') with its order varied to give LISK.

Fifthly, anagrams or part-anagrams may be made even more difficult when the clue gives, instead of the word(s) of the anagram itself, *synonyms* for those words. Like this:

'But is it material to prohibit a strange, *intense dislike*? (8)'

Answer: BARATHEA – BAR/A/THEA. Here the whole answer is the 'material' in the clue. It's built up thus: BAR ('prohibit') + A + THEA ('intense dislike' in the clue = 'hate', and that's the word which when written out in 'strange' fashion can become THEA).

Finally, we think that the very best kind of anagram clue is that where the *same words* combine the anagram itself *and* the instructions indicating that the clue is an anagram – as in this example:

'Spread with *speed, sir* (8)'

Answer: DISPERSE. Which means 'spread' and that same 'spread' roughly indicates that you've to spread around the letters of 'speed, sir' to get the answer.

You'll already have seen a few of the phrases in the clues above which indicate that an anagram is present – 'mangled', ‘gives’, ‘variety’, ‘perhaps’, ‘makes one’, ‘spread’. There are, literally, hundreds of such words and we couldn’t possibly give them all. But to give you fair warning about anagrams, we went through the crosswords in one *Sunday Times* book to discover just how many different anagram ‘signals’ we could find. The following list has got most of those ‘anagram-signal’ expressions in it – in alphabetical order too. But there are doubtless many more.

all over the place
altered
another shape
anyhow, anyway
arranged, arrangement

bad
become, becoming
bend, bending
bizarre
break, breaking out
broken
by redefinition

change(d)
chaos
chop(ped) up
clumsy, clumsily
cocktail (very useful if you can make it ‘gin cocktail’ in the clue – and you can, often, because lots of words end in or contain ‘ing’)
collapse(d)
comes to
confused, in confusion
construction, constructed
cracked up
crash(ed)
crazy, crazily
crumpled
crushed

damage(d)
different

disaster
disguise(d)
dish of
disorder(ed)
disposed, disposition
disturbed
drunk(en)
dug over

eccentric
engaged in
enough (to make)

far from smoothly
flaws, flawed
flustered
foolishly presented
for
fracas
from the

getting roughed up
given a face-lift

hotchpotch

in
in a bad way
in a heap
in(to) a new dish
incorrect(ly)
in knots
into pieces
involved

kind (of)
knocked into shape

mad, madly
mangled
maybe
melting-pot
misinterpret(ed)
mixed, mixture

muddle(d)

new
new-fangled
new order

odd(ly)
off
organize(d)
out
outcome
out of order

perhaps
poor(ly)
potential(ly)

rebuilt
recipe
refined
reform(ed)
reorganized
repaired
resolved, resolution
revolution
rewritten
riot, riotous
rocky
rough(ly)
ruin(ed)
run amok
running in

scattered, scattering
scruffy
shape(d)
shuffle(d)
slips into
smashed, smash up
sort (of)
spoilt
state of disrepair
storm

strange(ly)
stumbling
swirling
switches

thicket
throw
tip out
transporting
trouble(d)
turbulent
turn out (to be)
twisting

unorthodox
unruly
unusual(ly)
unusual dose
upset

variety
variously

went to pieces
wild(ly)
wobbly
woolly

e *'Contained-word' or hidden clues*

Clues sometimes give a hidden definition of the answer and also, literally, 'contain' the answer in the course of spelling out some of the words in the clue. The simplest way in which the compiler signals this is by words like 'in', 'of' or 'out of' in the clue. For example, 'Girl who goes out of Ber**lin da**ily'. Answer: LINDA; or, 'Comfort found in Chels**ea's e**legant houses'. Answer: EASE.

There are, as with anagrams, several words which can warn you of a 'contained-word', although they're certainly not as numerous as the anagram signals. They include 'from', 'part of', 'partially', 'falls into', and 'some of'. Here are some examples of 'contained-word' or 'split-word' clues and answers:

'Poet falls into the la**ke at S**alerno (5)'

Answer: KEATS.

'Delay one's departure from Ber**lin, Ger**many (6)'

Answer: LINGER.

'In this particular case, it's some of the star player**s at Chel**sea (7)'

Answer: SATCHEL.

'Used by a teach**er as er**uditely as possible (6)'

Answer: ERASER (note here that no definition of 'eraser' is included in the clue; one relies on the loose association of the fact that an 'eraser' is likely to be used by a teacher, to round out the clue).

f *'Sound-word' clues*

Part of the word play in cryptic crosswords is based on the fact that some words *sound* like others (e.g. 'Eton' sounds like 'eaten'; 'aroma' sounds like 'a roamer'). Again, the best way is to give examples – but you can often expect a 'sound' clue if a clue contains expressions like 'one hears', 'I hear', 'apparently', 'it seems', 'it appears', 'from the sound of it', and so on. Examples are these:

'One hears it's more disgusting, bitter resentment (7)'

Answer: RANCOUR. It means 'bitter resentment'; it sounds like 'ranker' ('more disgusting').

'Trousers are a source of quarrels, it seems (8)'

Answer: BREECHES (sounds like 'breaches').

'A really red-blooded bit of light opera, one hears (9)'

Answer: RUDDIGORE (sounds like 'ruddy gore').

'Sounds as if it goes on and on at the breakfast table (6)'

Answer: CEREAL (sounds like 'serial').

'Goes over the top with old tennis stars apparently (7)'

Answer: EXCEEDS (sounds like 'ex-seeds').

'Mark it for special attention apparently, with a label (6)'

Answer: TICKET (sounds like 'tick it').

g *Use of abbreviations*

Cryptic crossword clues are full of words spelt out fully, but whose role in building up the answer is that of an *abbreviation* only. Sometimes the clue indicates, by the use of phrases like 'small', 'minor', 'quickly', 'little', 'briefly', 'shortly', etc., that you are meant to abbreviate the word, but this is by no means always so. Frequently the solver has to deduce that an abbreviation is what's required in the answer or part-answer. Some examples of the use of abbreviations in clues:

'A heavyweight goes to *Alabama* for an unusual kind of music (6)'

Answer: ATONAL. A/TON/AL; AL = Alabama.

'Final message, by direction, is mature (4)'

Answer: RIPE. R.I.P./E; R.I.P. = requiescat in pace, rest in peace (thus, with word play, 'final message'); E = East ('direction').

'Crushed the publicity man first – that's what's offered for your consideration (10)'

Answer: PROPOUNDED. P.R.O./POUNDED; P.R.O. = public relations officer ('publicity man'), which comes 'first' before POUNDED ('crushed').

Abbreviations cover many pages in standard works of reference such as *Chambers' Twentieth Century Dictionary* and the *Concise Oxford Dictionary*, but to give you pointers to the huge variety which can be used, here is a list covering the most common of them.

AB	= able-bodied seaman ('sailor')
a/c a.c.	= account
AD	= anno domini ('our era', 'our time')
A1	= first-class (note that in cryptic crosswords the letter 'i' and the figure '1' are usually regarded as interchangeable; thus in a clue the letter 'i' may be rendered as 'one')
Al, Ala	= Alabama
a.m.	= morning
Au	= gold
BA	= Bachelor of Arts (loosely, 'bachelor', 'degree', etc.)

BA	= British Airways ('airline')
BOAC	= British Overseas Airways Corporation ('airline'). Old-fashioned usage now
Br.	= British, Britain, brother
C	= 100, Roman numeral (loosely 'many', 'a lot of'). Note also other Roman numerals like V = 5; VI = 6, half a dozen; X = 10; D = 500; M = 1000
CA	= chartered accountant
CE	= civil engineer, Church of England (strictly speaking, C of E)
CH	= Companion of Honour (loosely, 'honourable companion', 'award', 'honour', etc.)
co.	= company (loosely, 'firm', etc.)
cr.	= credit
D/d	= date, daughter, democrat, died, penny (as it once was – loosely, 'copper'), degree
DA	= District Attorney (thus 'US lawyer', etc.)
DD	= Doctor of Divinity (loosely, 'doctor')
dept	= department
Di	= Diana
Dr	= Doctor
ed.	= editor, edition
e.g.	= for example, for instance
enc.	= enclosure
EP	= extended play (loosely, 'record', 'disc')
f/ff	= forte (loosely, 'loud', 'strong', 'very loud', etc.)
Fri.	= Friday (cf. other days of the week – Sun., Mon., Tues., Wed., Thurs., Sat.)
Gen/gen.	= Genesis, general(ly)
i/c, i.c.	= in charge (of)
i.e.	= that is
IOM	= Isle of Man (loosely, 'Man')
IRA	= Irish Republican Army (loosely, 'illegal army', 'illegal organization', etc.)
Kt	= knight
L/l.	= learner (thus, loosely, 'beginner', 'novice', 'tyro', etc.), line, lira, licentiate, left
lab.	= laboratory (loosely, 'scientific centre', etc.)
Lab.	= Labour (loosely, 'politician')
Lib.	= Liberal (loosely, 'politician')

LP = long play(ing) (loosely, 'record', 'disc', etc.)
ma = mother (loosely, 'parent')
MA = Master of Arts (loosely, 'master', 'degree', etc.)
MB = Medicinae Baccalaureus – Bachelor of Medicine (loosely, 'doctor')
MO = Medical Officer (loosely, 'doctor')
MP = Member of Parliament (loosely, 'politician')
OBE = Officer of the Order of the British Empire (loosely, 'award', 'honour', 'order')
OS = outsize, very large
p/pp = piano (loosely, 'soft', 'quiet', etc.), participle
pa/Pa = father (loosely, 'dad', 'parent'), Pennsylvania
pro = in favour of (loosely, 'a person in favour of'), professional
PRO = Public Relations Officer (loosely, 'publicity man', etc.)
pt = point
R/Rt = right, royal
RA = Royal Artillery (loosely, 'gunner(s)', 'corps', etc.), Royal Academician (loosely, 'artist', 'painter')
re = about, concerning, with regard to, in the case of
RE = Royal Engineers (loosely, 'sapper(s)', 'engineer(s)', 'corps', etc.)
RI = Rhode Island
RMS = Royal Mail Ship (loosely, 'ship', 'liner', 'mail-boat', etc.)
RN = Royal Navy (loosely, 'navy', 'fleet', 'sailors', etc.)
RU = Rugby Union (i.e. Rugby football)
ry/rly = railway
S/s = second(s), shilling (former coin – hence, loosely, 'Bob', 'old Bob'), sister
SA = South Africa
Sal = Sarah
sis = sister
sop. = soprano
sp. = specialist
SP = starting-price (i.e. of a horse in a horse-race; loosely, 'final odds')

SS	= steamship (loosely, 'ship', 'liner')
St/st	= saint (loosely, 'holy man', etc.), street (loosely, 'highway', 'way', etc.)
tr.	= translator, translation
U	= upper class (loosely, 'socially acceptable'; cf. non-U)
UN	= United Nations (loosely, 'international organisation', 'international government', etc.)
US USA	= United States of America
Va	= Virginia

h *Disguise of verbs as nouns, nouns as verbs, etc.*

Clues will also try to make the solver believe that a particular part of speech should be read as a different part of speech. No rules can be made to cover this, but a few examples will illustrate what you face:

'Want hatred to crumble (6)'

Answer: DEARTH. 'Hatred' in the clue is its anagram (indicated by 'crumble') and its meaning is 'want' (noun) whereas the clue suggests it should be read as a verb.

'The most sensible like returning home (6)'

Answer: SANEST – SA/NEST. Here, 'like' suggests itself as a verb, but it isn't; it's an informal preposition, roughly equivalent to 'as' which you've to reverse ('like returning') to build up SA, the first part of the answer.

'Quiet husband left inside (5)'

Answer: SALVE – SA(L)VE. A real brute! 'Quiet' is a verb meaning 'to salve'; 'husband' is a verb too, meaning SAVE; 'inside' the word SAVE, place L (= 'left', abbreviation) and you get SALVE.

i *Puns and double meanings*

Again, you can't make rules about this, but since puns and double meanings are the heart and soul of cryptic crosswords, an explanation of some examples will serve as a guide:

'House a poet whilst making spanners (8, 7)'

Answer: BUILDING BRIDGES. A BUILDING could be a 'house'; BRIDGES is a 'poet' (Robert Bridges); and if you're

BUILDING BRIDGES you're 'making spanners' (i.e. objects that span).

'Performed by many willing people? (8)'

Answer: EXECUTED. People who carry out wills (i.e. 'willing people') are 'executing' wills.

'Heated singer! (6)'

Answer: KETTLE. Kettles 'sing' as they approach boiling point.

'Beloved and belobed? (8)'

Answer: ENDEARED – END/EARED. A gentle play on words since the 'lobes' are at the 'end' of the 'ears', so a coining is invented for the clue, 'belobed'.

'Could easily be standing in the view of others (8)'

Answer: PRESTIGE.

j *Overt or disguised references to literature, etc.*
A couple of examples:

'Land of Hope (9)'

Answer: RURITANIA. Remember 'Land of Hope and Glory, Mother of the Free'? Well, this has nothing to do with it – though the compiler hopes the solver will think it has! It's a reference to the novel *Prisoner of Zenda* by Anthony Hope, whose setting was the imaginary kingdom of Ruritania in Central Europe.

'Haggard heroine gets the record for mutton! (5)'

Answer: SHEEP – SHE/E.P. No, the heroine isn't haggard. The reference is to Rider Haggard's novel *She.* The 'record' is an E.P. (extended play).

k *Special crossword conventions*
You will have realised from the letters on 'Crossword Country' in *The Times* quoted on page 10 that cryptic crosswords have attracted to themselves a host of traditions and conventions. When a clue mentions the word 'degree', it's almost certain to be the letters 'MA' or 'BA' you're going to put in the answer somewhere. If it's a 'politician', you're looking for 'MP', or 'Lib', 'Lab', 'Soc' or 'Tory'. When 'parson' or 'minister' crops up, expect 'Rev'. The word 'gallery' should usually point you to 'Tate'. And you're going to turn 'the French' into 'le', 'la' or 'les'; 'the little devil' into 'imp'; 'love' into 'o' (that's tennis); and 'a beautiful young man' into 'Apollo'.

There are rather more subtle conventions which should be mentioned. The initials 'S S' stand for 'steamship', 'liner'. So a word like 'shops' might be clued, 'Jump in a ship to get stores' – S(HOP)S. Loosening up the clue further, it could read 'Jump on board to get stores'. When you see 'on board' in a clue it's an almost certain sign that the letters 'S——S' will be wrapped around something. Another convention is the use of the word 'initially', as in this clue: 'Old boy initially has a valet carefully attentive', to which the answer is OBSERVANT (O.B./SERVANT). 'Initially' indicates that you want the initial letters of 'old boy' as part of the solution.

Another convention. Come across the phrase 'with some hesitation' or 'hesitantly' or 'sound of hesitation' in a clue and the chances are that the letters 'er' or 'um' will be needed as a section of the answer. For instance:

'Second sound of hesitation creates the impetus (8)'

> *Answer:* MOMENTUM – MOMENT/UM. 'Second' = MOMENT; 'sound of hesitation' = UM.

'Without hesitation suffer anger in the vote (8)'

> *Answer:* SUFFRAGE – SUFF(ER)/RAGE. In this clue you've to *remove* the sound of hesitation (ER), as indicated by '*without* hesitation', from the clue word 'suffer'. That gives you SUFF to which you add RAGE ('anger').

To explain such conventions doesn't mean that crossword clues depend entirely on them by any means, nor that crosswords are full of clichés. But it's as well to know a few of the more common tricks of the trade. Here's a quick guide to some of them, with the likely word in the clue given *first*, and how it should be interpreted given on the right-hand side of the equation. The list includes some simple foreign words too:

a French = un, une
after the pattern of = in
all right = OK
alternative, alternative word = or
ancient city = Ur (Ur of the Chaldees)
at home = in
away, not at home = out
banker = river (i.e., something with banks)

bloomer	= flower (i.e., something that blooms; useful because 'bloomer' is slang for 'blunder')
by way of	= in
circle	= O
Communist	= Red
correct	= OK
dear French	= cher
direction	= N, S, E, or W
Edward (little Edward)	= Ted
first-class	= ai (A1)
flower	= river (i.e., something that flows!)
former	= ex
from foreign from French	= de
Henry (little Henry)	= Hal
in the fashion of in the style of	= à la
in the main	= in the sea
Irishman	= Pat
is French	= est
Jack	= knave (cards), sailor
key	= A, B, C, D, E, F, or G
kiss	= X
late	= ex
let it be, let it stand, don't change it, etc.	= stet
little way	= rd (road), st (street)
London district	= EC, WC, SW, etc.
love	= O
Mediterranean	= Med.
Muse	= Erato (usually!)
note	= A, B, C, D, E, F, or G
of foreign of French	= de
of the French	= du, des
one	= i
one-time	= ex
piper's son	= Tom

quarter	= SW, NW, NE, SE, etc.
revolutionary	= red
Richard (little Richard)	= Dick
ring	= O
same	= idem, id.
said in France says in France	= dit
Scotsman	= Ian
spot marker	= X (viz.: 'X marks the spot')
tea, tee	= T
the first letter	= alpha
the French	= le, la, les
the French dance	= bal
the French sea the sea abroad	= mer
the Italian	= il
the last letter	= omega
the last word	= amen
the Spanish	= el
30-second	= min. (i.e., half a *min*ute; confusing since 'min' can also represent 'minute', being the official abbreviation for the word)
this French	= ce
Tom	= cat
unknown quantity	= X
very French	= très
wall abroad	= mur
was in the van	= led
way (e.g. 'in a way')	= rd (road), st (street)
who in France	= qui
writer	= pen
yes abroad yes in Germany	= ja

1 *Quotations*
In these, you simply have to fill in the missing word, which is indicated by a space left in the clue – thus:

'The quality of——is not strain'd' (*The Merchant of Venice*) (5)

Answer: MERCY

3 Specimen Puzzle

And finally, to give beginners, or relative beginners, a clear idea of how one particular puzzle is solved, here is a sample crossword, filled in as it would be on completion, with the clues and explanations of those clues. The number of letters in the answer is given in parentheses at the end of each clue.

Across

1 Cooler on the road, but warmer in the house (8)
5 Spanish fish seen in clouds of flying water (6)
9 How to carry baby – or is that revolting? (2, 2, 4)
10 Water-spirit in nude perhaps (6)
12 He's not treated in an honourable way! (6)
13 Was destroyed by means of one storage structure (8)
15 Grassy area on which a sporting gesture is made with bias! (7-5)
18 For each exciting experience in ancient times, perhaps (12)
23 They cut off ships (8)
24 All-rounder turning over an afterthought in this place? (6)
26 Maybe the singer is boss (6)
27 Town that certainly *ought* to be shown on a relief map (8)
28 Importance of acquiring some piastres suddenly (6)
29 Expedients in poetic metres? (8)

Down

1 Manhandles hoodlums (6)
2 Condescends to change the design (6)
3 A girl I love beside the seaside abroad! (7)
4 Resistance units working for the Queen . . . (4)
6 . . . using sharp steel against her husband in the act of stabbing! (7)

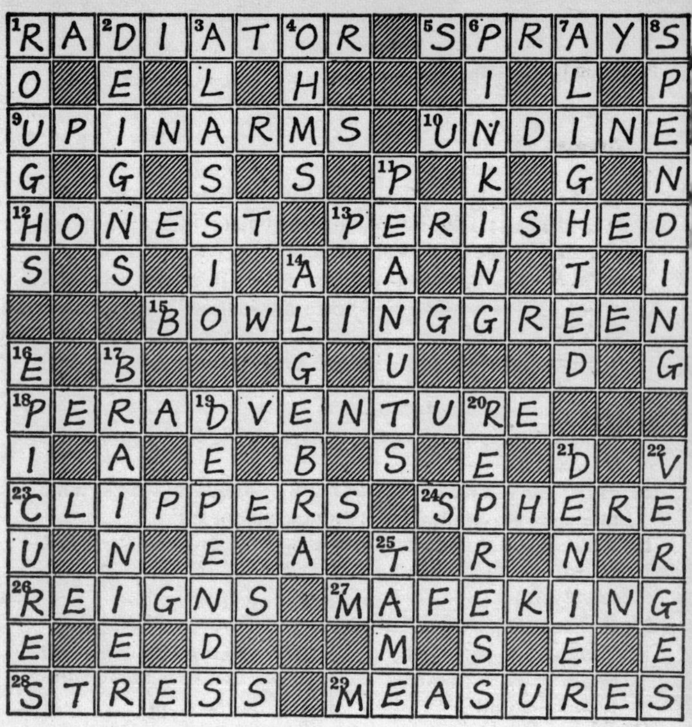

7 Didn't stay on to arrange a deal about some kind of pointless thing (8)
8 Series not yet decided? Exhausting, isn't it? (8)
11 Sent up a mixed bag of monkey food (7)
14 Symbolically calculating approach to problems (7)
16 Naturally they'll go for pure ices, won't they? (8)
17 Almost entirely princely, and altogether more clever (8)
19 Relies for support in trusts (7)
20 About to squeeze and put down (7)
21 One who refuses to admit the fineness of the stocking? (6)
22 Inclines to being Dogberry's partner? (6)
25 Mincemeat is so uninspiring (4)

Notes on the Answers

Across

1 RADIATOR is a play on words; a 'radiator' is a 'warmer' (i.e. a heater) in the home, but in a vehicle (indicated by 'on the road' in the clue) it's a cooling agent (i.e. a 'cooler')

5 SPRAYS: the meaning of the whole is 'clouds of flying water'; you build it up via SP (= 'Spanish', abbreviation) + RAYS (= 'fish')

9 UP IN ARMS means 'revolting' (i.e. in a state of revolt). The phrase can also loosely signify 'how to carry baby' – a clue involving word play

10 UNDINE, a 'water-spirit'; anagram, 'in nude', indicated by 'perhaps'

12 HONEST means 'honourable'; anagram, 'he's not', indicated by 'treated (in an honourable way)'

13 PERISHED means 'was destroyed'; built up by PER (= 'by means of') + I (= 'one') + SHED (= 'storage structure')

15 BOWLING-GREEN is a play on words; BOWLING-GREEN is the 'grassy area'; the bowls used are weighted so that they roll with a bias (which can also mean 'prejudice', and that forms the basis of the word play)

18 PERADVENTURE means 'perhaps', archaic – and, hence, the clue says 'in ancient times'. Built up with PER (= 'for each') + ADVENTURE (= 'exciting experience')

23 CLIPPERS means both 'ships' and 'cutting instruments', hence 'they cut off' in the clue, a play on words

24 SPHERE is indicated in the clue by 'all-rounder' (word play for a 'round' or 'globular' object). Built up by SP (= PS reversed, i.e. 'turning over' PS; PS means 'postscriptum' or, as the clue has it, 'afterthought', a slight word play) + HERE (= 'in this place')

26 REIGNS means 'is boss' (i.e. is predominant, has power); anagram, 'singer', indicated by 'maybe'

27 MAFEKING: word play on Mafeking, the South African town, the relief of which was so notable an incident in the Boer War

28 STRESS is a 'contained-word' clue. STRESS = 'importance', and to get the answer you have to 'acquire a certain amount of' the phrase 'pia**stres s**uddenly'

29 MEASURES means both 'expedients' and 'poetic metres', a simple example of a double-meaning or double-synonym clue

Down

1 ROUGHS means both 'manhandles' and 'hoodlums', another double-meaning clue

2 DEIGNS means 'condescends'; anagram, 'design', as indicated by 'to change'

3 ALASSIO is an Italian seaside resort, hence, 'beside the seaside abroad'. The build-up is A LASS (= 'a girl') + I (= 'I') + O (= 'love', the famous tennis parallel, in which 'love' means 'zero', '0' in scoring)

4 OHMS is given as 'resistance units' in the clue, which begins the word play (OHM is 'a unit of electrical resistance'). OHMS is also, of course, the abbreviation for On Her Majesty's Service (i.e. 'working for the Queen'). This clue is allowed to run on (. . .) simply because it links neatly with the next clue, a common cryptic crossword convention

6 PINKING means 'the act of stabbing'. Built up with PIN (= 'sharp steel') + (i.e. 'against') KING (= 'her husband', meaning the queen's husband)

7 ALIGHTED – the clue indicates this by 'didn't stay on' (i.e. got off). The build-up is AL(IGHT)ED – anagram, 'deal', indicated by 'to arrange', which is placed 'about' anagram, 'thing', indicated by 'some kind of', minus the letter 'n' (point of the compass – hence 'pointless thing' in the clue)

8 SPENDING is given as 'exhausting' in the clue; built up by S (= abbreviation for 'series') + PENDING (= 'not yet decided')

11 PEANUTS is 'monkey food' in the clue; anagram, 'sent up a', indicated aptly by 'mixed bag of'

14 ALGEBRA is a play on words; algebra uses symbols to work out arithmetical (hence, association with 'calculating') problems

16 EPICURES is an anagram, 'pure ices', indicated by 'go for'; the clue not requiring a strict definition of 'epicures', since such people would certainly only go for *pure* ices

17 BRAINIER means 'more clever'; built up by (B)RAINIER (i.e. Prince Rainier, hence, 'princely', Rainier forming 'almost entirely' the word required)

19 DEPENDS is a double-meaning clue; answer means 'relies for support' and 'trusts' (verb)

20 REPRESS means (to) 'put down'; constructed with RE (= 'about', i.e. regarding, concerning) + (indicated by 'to', i.e. joined to) PRESS (= 'squeeze')

21 DENIER is a word play with a double meaning: 'one who refuses to admit' and 'fineness of stocking'

22 VERGES means 'inclines (to)'; Verges was Dogberry's partner (a fellow town-constable) in Shakespeare's *Much Ado About Nothing*

25 TAME means 'uninspiring' (i.e. insipid, lacking interest); anagram, 'meat', as aptly indicated by 'mincemeat'

ELIZABETH AND DEREK JEWELL

The Puzzles

1

Across

1 Manicurists' manual? (8)
5 Rises to obtain drink (4, 2)
9 Boxer and another dog I enter for the record (8)
10 Senior lady is a bit taken aback when there's a chap around (6)
12 Recording is out of key (6)
13 Hit and run? That's careless! (8)
15 Cleanest side – that's where the cooked meats are sold (12)
18 Is not solaced, maybe (12)
23 Working in the foundry, crumbles, decaying (8)
24 Perhaps a start for the layers (6)
26 In the ranks, we see colourful neckwear (6)
27 Cocoa's in order for the party (8)
28 Local authority levy on a sailor? (6)
29 Where to purchase cheap Chinese vessels? (4-4)

Down

1 Wanting to stick something sharp into the pig? (6)
2 Points to the way in – only to say it's not there! (6)
3 It weighs whatever is left over (7)
4 Duck on purpose in the river (4)
6 No longer stout and is now a model (7)
7 Sea that's full of weed – has gas in it too (8)
8 There's taste in this swansong (8)
11 Pay bill in flexible fashion (7)
14 French leader is certain to crack (7)
16 Motored East by a diversion, getting instrument for the cab (8)
17 Luce seen squirming in nets cast out will be good to eat (8)
19 One of last year's runners? (3, 4)
20 A bird or two (7)
21 Disappear just as transport is going to the hospital (6)
22 Fall unconscious briefly, due to insect turning up inside hat (3-3)

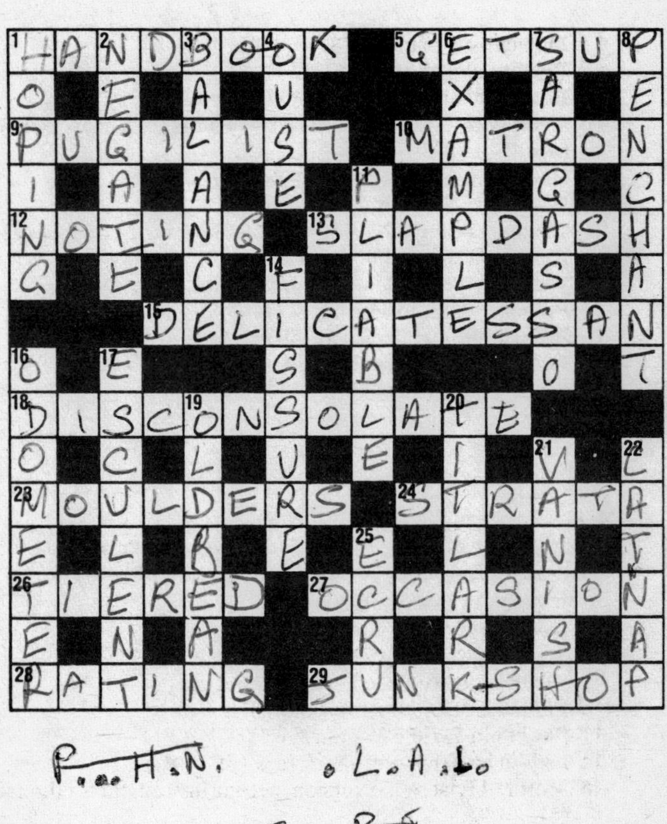

25 It's greyish-yellow inside the cruet (4)

2

Across

4 Guide has a lot of time for economy travel (8)
8 Drag used in river in flood (6)
9 Opinion held about folk in a slum dwelling (8)
10 He was expected to have a second helping (8)
11 In disarray, sits to an artist (6)
12 Put down, for example, in recount (8)
13 An oil-rig at sea – the prototype (8)
16 Drawing liquor before the troops get at it (8)
19 Devise means of obtaining access to the cargo (8)
21 Girl on a horse with tail docked (6)
23 Road with right turn bad to get across (8)
24 Has print-out to pass on, craftily (8)
25 Unanimous about having to be among the senescent (6)
26 Tutor set out to be on the box (3-5)

Down

1 Held place in the rush (7)
2 Sea diver with pangs of conscience, having eaten most of the fruit (9)
3 In the eye or near it (6)
4 Decide where to go and pay right away (6, 2, 3, 4)
5 Expert on figures – a product of the naughty nineties (8)
6 Twin river birds (5)
7 In which to travel to a town in Zambia? (7)
14 Completely baffled as to how the lamp works? (2, 3, 4)
15 In addition, going into Sunday School, use the scraper for footwear (4-4)
17 Watch what you say (7)
18 Youngster getting a rise is deceitful and wastes time (7)
20 Unusual dearth of clue? (6)
22 Repent the devil an oral interpretation of these symbols (5)

2

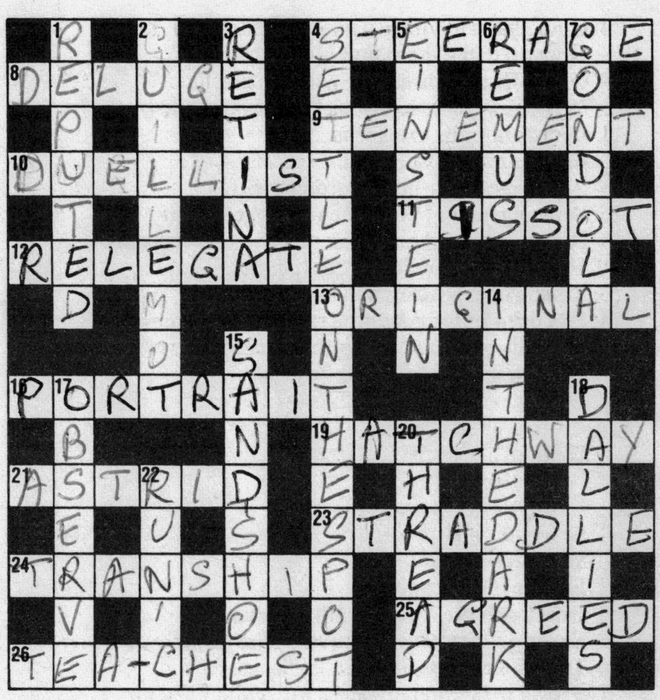

3

Across

1 Equally healthy, and a good thing too! (4, 2, 4)
6 Recognize the listener may get a rebuff (4)
9 Make off-peak calls (5)
10 Writer forming part of the chain eventually (9)
12 Girl frightened she's lost a letter – someone with thieving habits around? (5-8)
14 The drink is finished – it's ominous (8)
15 Seedy painter? (6)
17 A fitting hat for the garden (6)
19 Presentation company report gets into papers – an embarrassing situation (8)
21 Had I a pattern I could adapt for togetherness (4-9)
24 Sand-storm devastated place and all that's in it as far as the eye can see (9)
25 I'm taking a shot at a butterfly (5)
26 Call for help love – it's only fair (2-2)
27 Created a disturbance – but schoolmaster prepared to deal with it, we hear (6, 4)

Down

1 Birds with eyes in front, it's said (4)
2 Seating manufacturer displays this kind of seal (7)
3 Lodger has gate damaged in dispute (2, 11)
4 Prosperous water engineer with work lined up (4-2-2)
5 Object hidden in the chest I conclude must be clothing (5)
7 The sort of history that's only to be expected (7)
8 Those who tend to carry them out aren't politically orientated (4, 6)
11 No longer a leader in the field of heat conservation? (7, 6)
13 Contraption crossing the bridge (10)
16 Additional strengthening needed, there being some doubt over the lock (8)
18 Circle fashionable square and sing drunkenly on these occasions? (7)

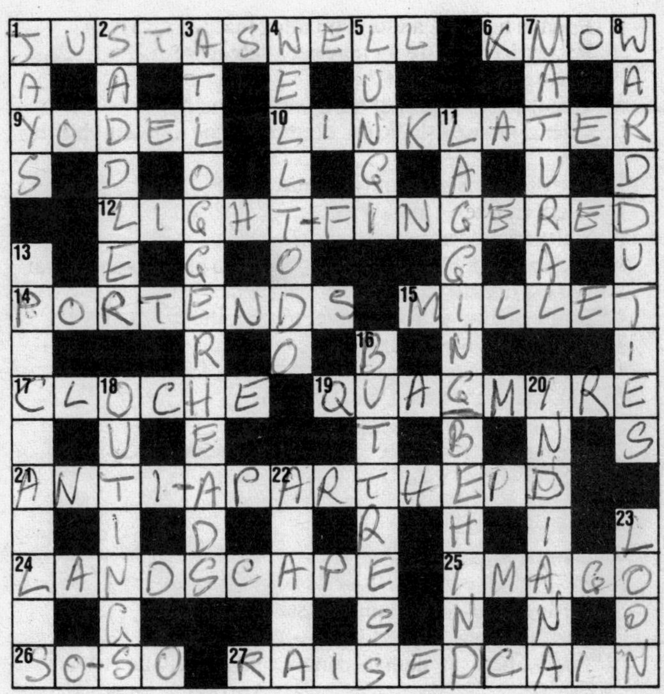

20 Country surrounding an American state (7)
22 Reptile disclosed when a magazine is turned over (5)
23 Half-witted bird? (4)

4

Across

1 Tin opener no good if holding wine sampling party (7)
5 May stumble upon a wilful piece of treachery (7)
9 Duck egg the pilot has eaten could be the death of him (7)
10 Ringing painter back to cancel arrangement (7)
11 In the glen faces tingle in confusion at surreptitious peeps (8, 7)
12 One islander is here and the rest ran off (6)
14 Irregular triangle could be complete in itself (8)
17 Product of inferior marksmanship (8)
18 Set a speed about fifty and was one of the first to finish (6)
21 Every cent paid me gets a formal acknowledgement (7, 8)
24 Putting on the scaffolding (7)
25 Keep taking notice (7)
26 Lad gone off somewhere over the water (7)
27 Tank full of the green stuff? (7)

Down

1 Jam-making trade? (7)
2 One's fated, perhaps, to be like a granite post? (5-4)
3 What an ass – I'd nothing invested in it (5)
4 Places for putting vegetables (6)
5 Passing from one state to another, is caught and strung up (8)
6 Just one of the hundreds and thousands – yet it's unique (9)
7 Priest in church is a bit of a saint (5)
8 Attendance to the books can give endless pleasure (7)
13 Give chain, fashioned specially, as an award for success? (9)
15 Felt better and got dressed again (9)
16 Anxious Gaul after haven in the country (8)
17 Was against work and just sat (7)
19 Wouldn't work at all – gone off in a huff (7)
20 Air travellers circling North shore (6)

22 Only the beginning and end of yarn absorb the listener – it's long (5)
23 With no difficulty, a beginner can take pictures (5)

5

Across

1 Foot discovered by two boys is source of many fantastical tales of derring-do (9, 6)
9 Provides overhead protection from the rain (4-3)
10 Ascribes dishonourable conduct as reason for being placed in semi-retirement (7)
11 Skirting trouble at the back of beyond (4)
12 From this road, darts out – crashes! A A must be involved (10)
13 A log hit him? As the story went, it was a stone (7)
15 By the Red Sea, going into the water I tread warily (7)
17 Cause humbling of French papers (7)
19 Has wings and flies for our entertainment (7)
20 Individual claiming to be of the cloth is manifestly spiritual (10)
22 Singer very keen to make a return appearance (4)
25 Show pleasure to this degree when bearing is out? (7)
26 Almost in heaven, flying to this place (7)
27 Darkness has cost the exchange much of its business (6, 3, 6)

Down

1 Bug took most of the sap and concealed itself (5)
2 It's not the first mistake the man in the field has made (5, 4)
3 Foul-natured cannibal holding a human bone (4)
4 Close to it, though not in play (2, 5)
5 Unpleasant rejection is nothing to me (7)
6 Time phase problem, when you need to fully integrate with another (9)
7 Player providing more than is required? (5)
8 Mixed pairs in time become beyond compare (9)
13 Supreme virtue of what the actor wants heard in the gallery (9)
14 Overcome with fear at perilously weak crust (3-6)
16 Terrier vet docked turns out to be quite fetching (9)

18 Quarter mile around the lake, a crane can be spotted (7)
19 Given the expertise, make a notch when climbing in the open air (7)
21 Musical top boy found in cracker (5)
23 The Ambassador gets aboard a ship and remains (5)
24 Isolated part of the foot (4)

6

Across

1 Reaction to the cat? (8)
5 Concerned with wild life and finding the difference between higher and lower levels (6)
9 Records of leading saint (8)
10 Ultimate letter hostile organization sent round is the catalyst (6)
12 Played its part when unreliable jumbo put down the day before? (6)
13 Superfluous trimming but not quite enough for elbow ruff (8)
15 Dress largely misfitting – it's made without care (12)
18 Reject the offer of a crib but leave it half-open, ready for use (4, 4, 1, 3)
23 Gloomily, see painter about a study group (8)
24 Slow-moving female I go round (6)
26 I skate round book – it holds work to be done (2-4)
27 Cover blown! Ring me then beat it (8)
28 Point taken down so just loose ends to be tied up (6)
29 Everything's affected by inflation but there's no need to worry (4, 4)

Down

1 Leaves iron marks on the wool, perhaps (6)
2 Small firms go forward in this case (6)
3 In France, the one certain time for relaxation (7)
4 Greek god raised, in port (4)
6 English apprentice turns up with French maid, to improve his status (7)
7 In such a wind, only bicycle front wheels keep going (3, 5)
8 Uninhibited behaviour apparently not taking toll of travellers abroad (8)
11 Old timer unable to work when the weather's bad (7)
14 Tom's former hunting ground – this path (3-4)
16 Stable charge for the occupant (8)

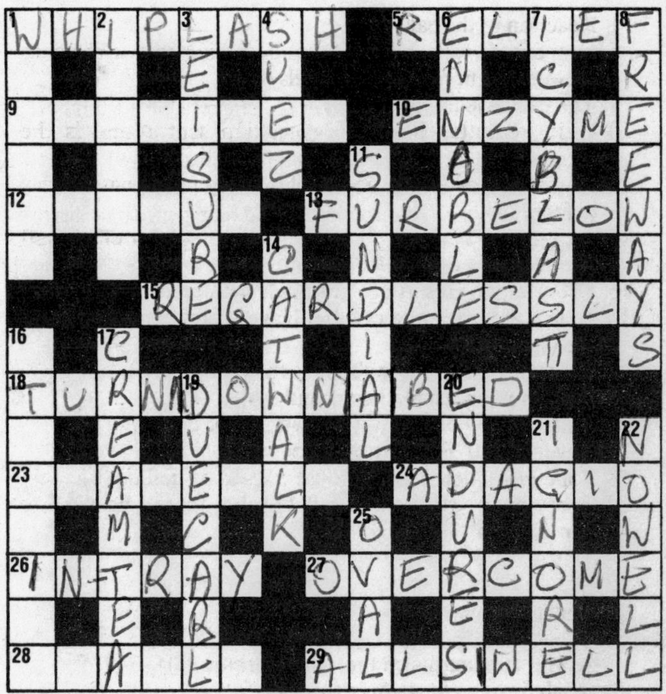

17 Team race abandoned in favour of an afternoon treat (5, 3)
19 The proper attention given by milkmaids to their complexions, it's said (3, 4)
20 Carries on patiently being certain, perhaps, to finish first (7)
21 No notice is required should you wish to do it (6)
22 Christmas present with the letter, we are told (6)
25 Like an egg? Here, there could be ducks (4)

7

Across

1 Drug a doctor took (8)
5 Left in carriage and pair (6)
9 Metallic element of fruit taken out of a can (8)
10 Half the embrocation used in the cricket club's from here? (6)
12 Accommodation once intended for spinsters? (5)
13 Patronized by readers wanting to reserve a seat (9)
14 He'll show benevolence with it and help orphan in distress (12)
18 Ambiguously giving a description of how an egg is formed (12)
21 The pathos of hungry animal pressing against effeminate young man (9)
23 Lists a near-riot (5)
24 Charm the stubborn by teasing, initially (6)
25 Nurse going round in what is left (8)
26 English loch side (6)
27 Pack needs cards dealt from it, the sailor found (8)

Down

1 Spiritless doctor to pooh-pooh (6)
2 Princess has poorly made crown (6)
3 Cooks large bone I found in position at the head (9)
4 A colossal number on the excursion to see the fireworks (12)
6 Makes eyes go back to front (5)
7 Write label attached to figure (8)
8 Did very well, the discharged prisoner? (8)
11 Secured with ropes to a railway track? It's the limit! (8, 4)
15 Brief moment in which part of the insect becomes visible (4, 1, 4)
16 Hold liquor as a memento (8)
17 A titled union leader manoeuvred into high position (8)
19 The girl is out of breath (6)

20 Feeling aroused by the sort of trick with which an anarchist is linked (6)
22 Girl indicating direction that is taken by the engineer (5)

8

Across

1 Trots on in a trap – an alternative way of covering the distance (14)
10 Some guts required, to take to the stage with no backing (7)
11 So hard to be a mother and also a worker (7)
12 Heavy levers required for quite a small quantity of ingots (9)
13 Swift characters, these brutes (5)
14 Tax on car that would not pass its MOT comes as rather a choker (6)
15 An Arab, he gets thrown out of a dance in Cuba (8)
18 Peep at it miserably, longing for it (8)
20 Athletic Club a spy organization? It's a plant (6)
23 Have a snooze in it, though it's not appropriate (5)
25 Nocturnal fragrance apparently bringing on drowsy numbness (9)
26 Not quite right in earlier performance (7)
27 1 across, for example, providing vital link for divers (7)
28 Teenager seeking cheap lodgings is shocked by those let hourly (5-9)

Down

2 Many gallons of ale in road, swirling round building (7)
3 Where that snore might come from (5-4)
4 State the joke has thrust (6)
5 Raises the fare, after removing a quarter of passenger accommodation (4, 4)
6 There's lack of co-ordination always shown, on receiving a levy (5)
7 Novel Russian farming aid (7)
8 Country air? (8, 6)
9 Show deference to talent – socially it's an asset (14)
16 Coming down from Lancaster by a roundabout route (9)
17 High heel that makes toes tilt perilously (8)
19 High-rise flat in the countryside (7)

8

21 Garment I scheme to replace (7)
22 Maps lead to square, eventually (2, 4)
24 All the thief would find in his purse, Iago declares (5)

9

Across

1 Just a trifle left (7)
5 Lifted on high from under a tree (7)
9 The fault is acerbated by an ulcer (7)
10 New part-conversion of old port (7)
11 A coy dimple which isn't shown up by a smile from one in this mood (5, 10)
12 Pole was none too well pinned down (6)
14 Order a fruit dessert (5, 3)
17 Caught getting warmed up and that's breaking the rules! (8)
18 In first set, see how ball flies! (6)
21 Heart hurt wee Ned, doctor – he's still far from well (5, 3, 7)
24 State in the manner of one graduate receiving his senior (7)
25 Fricassee of rib chop traditionally on the menu at Hogmanay (7)
26 She's of the lean or athletic build (7)
27 Hide the ring in the escritoire at home (3-4)

Down

1 Give up what may well be a burden (7)
2 Alien scum, maybe, but this doesn't refer to the ladies (9)
3 Piercing accent? (5)
4 Ammunition in the architect's office (6)
5 Parties travelling south, cruising (3-5)
6 A crew from Avon will add that touch of luxury to the tub (4, 5)
7 Old Celts might have been nice, I understand (5)
8 The money involved in keeping swans in a river (7)
13 Provide a diversion in harbour (9)
15 To get one attuned to work on the farm? (5-4)
16 Undecided, I then change the tune (2, 3, 3)
17 Fortitude's needed to face the cold at our time of life (7)
19 Made of clay from Teheran (7)

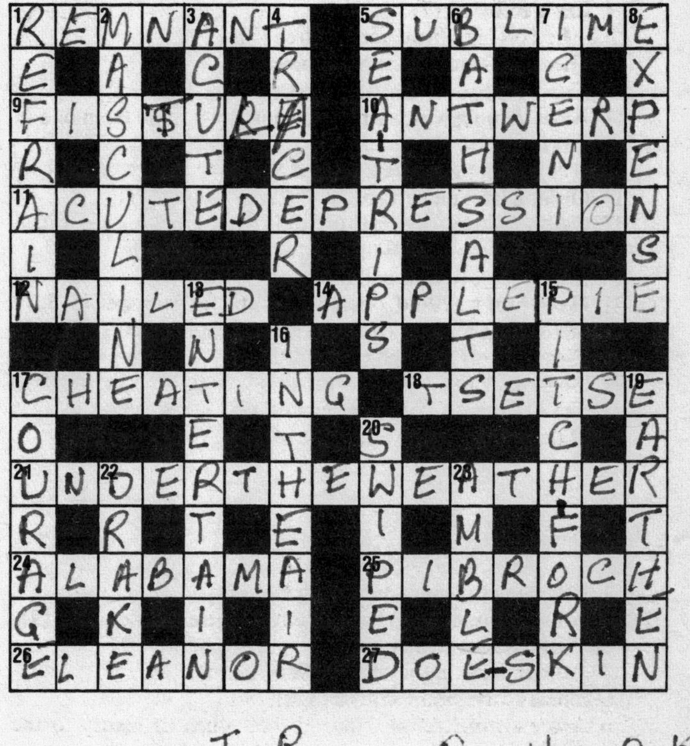

20 Lashed out and made a quick trip around the West Indies (6)
22 Sailor who was naturally at home on the water? (5)
23 Doctor in his cups in no hurry to walk this way (5)

10

Across

4 Without transport, going round the orient? So slapdash! (8)
8 Attack the woman this way (6)
9 Hard it is, to convert a doubter (8)
10 Bogus diamond – it's a plant! (8)
11 This long-distance runner is a formidable woman (6)
12 Called the game off, as some did at the border crossing (8)
13 It's no act – it needs treatment, this yawning (8)
16 Shelled below the waterline (8)
19 Part of breakaway group that may come from the wood (8)
21 Head directed to good book that's open (6)
23 Exclusion of nothing on purpose (8)
24 Battle station (8)
25 Players appearing one by one (6)
26 Holy man needs to hedge, to seem favourable to both sides (8)

Down

1 Vessel with reduced tonnage (7)
2 Camouflage expert could make home clean (9)
3 Protection for king caught in intriguing situation (6)
4 Put paid to your plan for keeping the bird alive? (6, 4, 5)
5 A dancer and I waltzing in the moonlight (8)
6 Grub penetrating right into volcanic rock (5)
7 Tennis score put in writing (3, 4)
14 Shine dart badly dulled (9)
15 Dashed, having been made to go to the bottom (8)
17 Girl meets chap coming up to the junction but doesn't give way (7)
18 Study circle boy joined as indicated (7)
20 Stand about, just to rile constituents (6)
22 Key workers coming up with a means of flushing internal piping (5)

10

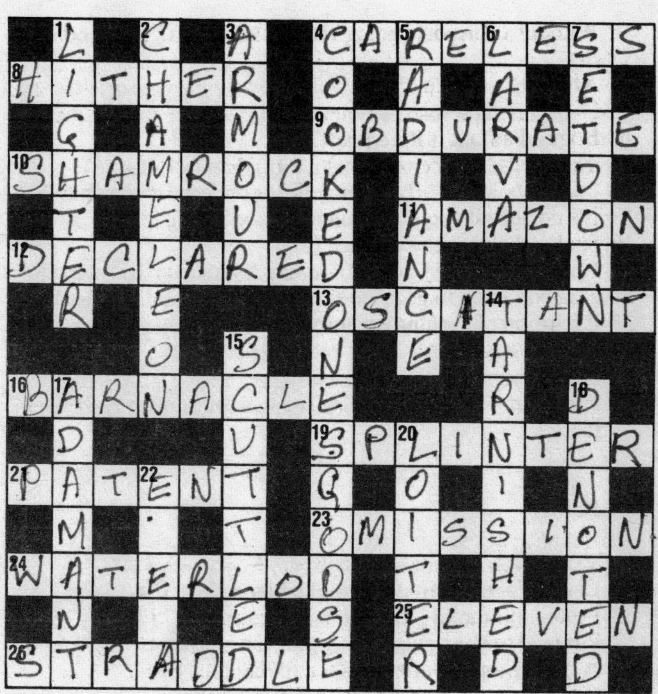

11

Across

1 Drunken Australian orgy (10)
8 Fatuous to censor article (4)
10 Marginally altered? To a quite frightening degree! (10)
11 Prove undependable? Not my family! (4)
13 Chunks of two different fruits in the salad (7)
15 Come to a halt in a main road? (6)
16 Some nameless ingredient ensures the smooth finish (6)
17 Wood elf or goblin? Could be! (5, 10)
18 Save to pay off the loan (6)
20 The kind of bullet used to get the sleuth (6)
21 Can't decide whether or not to take this red mixture (7)
22 Capital punishment for five in foreign country (4)
25 Heedless of obstacles, its owner drives on (4, 2, 4)
26 He takes a very long time inserting the last letter (4)
27 With fresh fervour et cetera, set out for foreign shores (3, 7)

Down

2 Just a gentle touch, exposing the palm (4)
3 Raised specifically for use as an arrow poison (4)
4 An issue that's less sensitive now (6)
5 The potential of policemen doing a stretch? (4, 3, 2, 3, 3)
6 Assert a point in legal wrangle (6)
7 More attractive in bed than at the ball? (10)
9 It's rousing and may carry lots of clout initially, an early riser holds (5-5)
12 Drive a bus carelessly over the key and you need him! (5, 5)
13 Set off on grey, perhaps (7)
14 Aims to captivate the listener and is successful, it appears (7)
15 Neatly coiffed Cockney, painted in explosive style (3-7)
19 Small type – wearing a short skirt (6)
20 Play with only a small amount (6)
23 Has a speaking role in a Morality play (4)
24 Article to forward shortly (4)

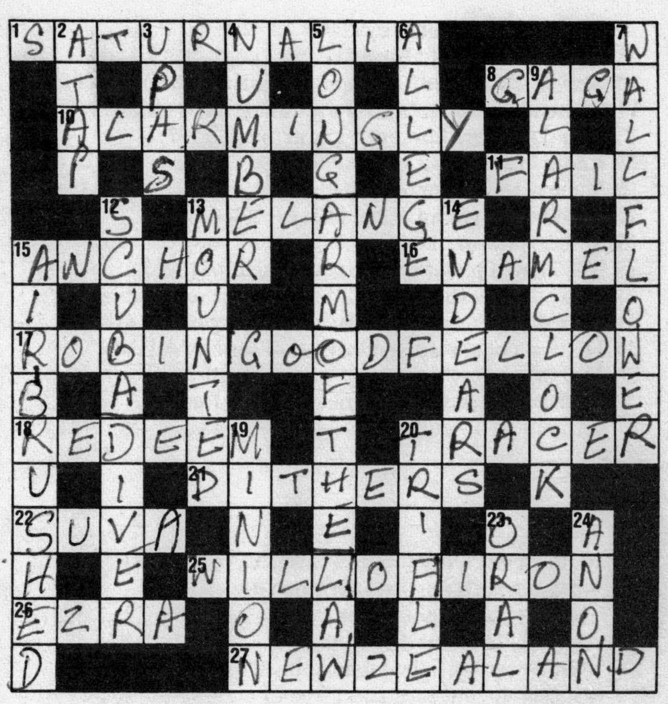

12

Across

1 Start fishing for something that makes a clicking sound (8)
5 Sauce sat fermenting in small open container (6)
9 Found the cure – but it was too late to help the engineer (8)
10 Rambling, extravagant speech delivered by Her Majesty (6)
12 It explains how more than one person goes out or in (6)
13 Manage without make up (8)
15 Somehow, I can't use this with much interest (12)
18 Metal worker making part of the orchestra break down (12)
23 Assistance spurned prior to territorial group making violent attack (8)
24 Take things for granted, like birds flying backwards (6)
26 Revolutionary diet – half a worm – for literary man (6)
27 Young foreign medico one left inside (8)
28 Perhaps it's a retrograde measure, for drink (6)
29 Carry on, with support (8)

Down

1 A hint about renegade church official (6)
2 Time of year when the adder can be seen (6)
3 Stand by the fire also at the club (7)
4 Jug animal and roast initially (4)
6 Roman general sounds likely to have held on with determination (7)
7 Agents at work to become unproductive (8)
8 A game of cards needed by the waiters (8)
11 Opposition vote is posted following day (7)
14 Instrument with which we bring the cycle of time to nothing (7)
16 Following instructions, be on diet that's nasty (8)
17 Ram a vessel heading for the islands (8)
19 Somewhat less than a baron of beef (7)
20 Point behind the ship towards the sunrise (7)
21 Expected girl to turn up with chaperon (6)

22 Magician's bird (6)
25 Old ruler one can replace (4)

13

Across

1 Novel character of the bird preserve (9, 6)
9 Arraign one member apiece (7)
10 Dial – as planned (4, 3)
11 Banker featuring in three Brontë novels (4)
12 Goad an unbeliever into making partisan statements (10)
13 Throw out a proposal (7)
15 The stuff one expects to give (7)
17 Make a hoax call – you've caught fellow handling fake Lowry (3, 4)
19 The only one with an overdraft put on a new footing (7)
20 Dash to record our years on earth (10)
22 Return to the Parisian look (4)
25 I call round on pressing business (7)
26 Supplies fruit or vegetable (7)
27 Pliant as the hare and with the suppleness of a cat running wild (5, 2, 1, 7)

Down

1 The best part to paint first (5)
2 Form of company stock (9)
3 It's something that might bite you, when seaweed is turned over (4)
4 Succeed in getting a woman to take it on (7)
5 English pupils hurling pies, in form (7)
6 Fishy essence all ready for drinking? (9)
7 Kelvin, on turning up, was not initially recognized (5)
8 Abstraction ultimately gets you transported (9)
13 Rigorous training for the poor dealer? (4-5)
14 Is one come to ruin, for failure to do this? (9)
16 Signal when obstruction comes up, for example, then strike at the centre (9)
18 Makes military incursions, getting in scrap with enemies (7)
19 Four characters leave reggae band? Take this advice! (7)
21 So hot it may be fire (5)

23 Duck about to drown after turning turtle (5)
24 Survey in metres (4)

14

Across

1 Bizarre decorations though each is in harmony with its neighbour (11).
10 One of the nerves we see twitch, after work (5)
11 Group activity in which one dissipates power a lot (5-4)
12 Princess, traveller, the Queen and I left in gravest danger (4, 5)
13 Winter hail – send me back south! (5)
14 Knotted loop fixed round delinquent's head (6)
16 She's quick to take offence and determined to get mince pie first (8)
18 Emergency treatment needed to make Christmas tree steady (5, 3)
20 Bark extract put girl in the money (6)
23 He has to be seen in hooded red gown, ermine-trimmed (5)
24 Head of fish – gift-wrapped (9)
26 Folk (Father Time excluded) who may be ordered to eat greens (9)
27 Trunk going to railway sorting office (5)
28 Our tart's mince – key part of the Christmas meal (5, 6)

Down

2 Oil turning to a thick viscid substance (5)
3 Instructions to provide about a hundred mince pies (7)
4 I have pulled up inside (6)
5 The beast has to run, after Etna eruption (8)
6 A pierced ear, maybe, for good hearing (7)
7 Words decidedly lacking in warmth are hidden in card Tony folds (4, 3, 6)
8 An unconventional type, King Wenceslas (8)
9 One cannot stir? This can give rise to feelings of alarm (13)
15 Common bats made the noise in the belfry – act to contain it! (8)
17 Draw crowd with this gadget – good present for dad? (3-5)
19 Rent trouble in the wind (7)

14

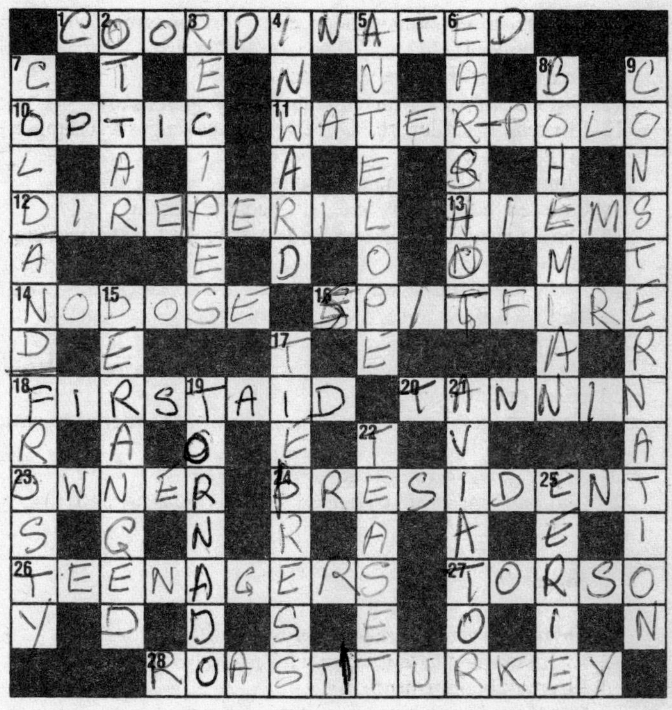

21 Obviously he found a way to rise initially (7)
22 China perhaps calling for redistribution of estate (3-3)
25 No head on the beer – that is strange! (5)

15

Across

1 Classical musician needed to transcribe her opus (7)
5 He makes sure he gets his vacations (7)
9 What the dentist may well do to one (7)
10 Black cloth some branches carried for funerals (7)
11 Like the man's den it is unfortunately a poor local thing (15)
12 Listen distractedly, but register (6)
14 Use it and find gold? (8)
17 In the past an underground worker, he now conducts trials (8)
18 A track for climbers (6)
21 Though I have the green man's permission, on the curb I worry – if I do it I shan't be able to get back again (5, 3, 7)
24 State of troops retreating after Anzio's blown to smithereens (7)
25 Claim to be the piper but taking it turn about for the drums (7)
26 Swallows having fun with legs interlaced (7)
27 A superior type of assistant? (7)

Down

1 I'm able to see to a clue that's cryptic (7)
2 Insect sautéed in frying-pan? It's meant to be smoked (9)
3 Due to deviation from the right track, is held by terrorists (5)
4 Mountaineer's turn of phrase (6)
5 Convict having served his time because a high achiever (8)
6 Critics ring me up spoiling Sunday (9)
7 Tic he developed stems from his weakness for a cuppa (5)
8 Taking stock of the commander – a good man at heart (7)
13 Continental car's failed to finish – it's a jammed cylinder (5, 4)
15 The Roman capitals have great charm, so effective in presentation (9)

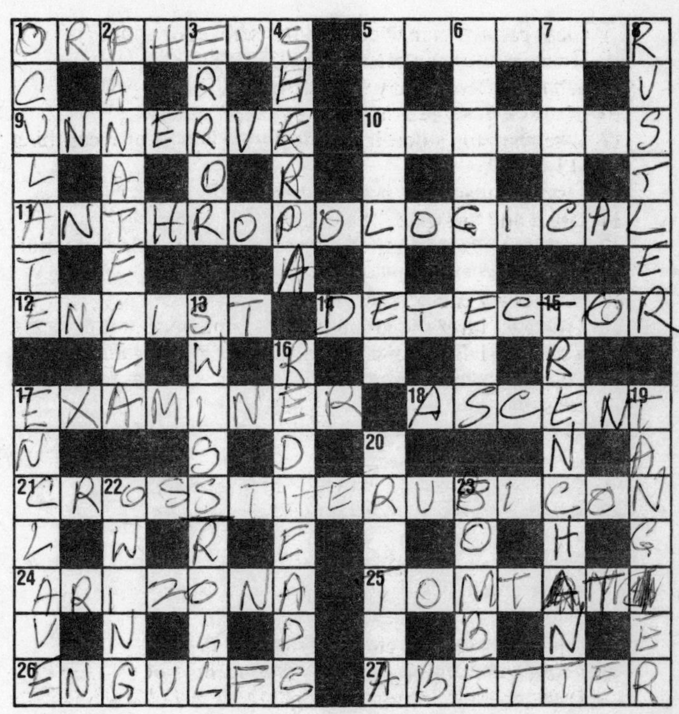

16 Blondes would not do for Communist bosses (3-5)
17 The previous night the gang turned out in the enclosure (7)
19 Comparatively pungent port (7)
20 Seed that's diseased can still produce a flower (6)
22 Due address to the flight commander (5)
23 The rabble brought up to exist on cold pudding (5)

16

Across

1 Keep flying? It's a fanciful notion (6, 2, 3, 3)
10 Demanding way-out, absorbing information (7)
11 Complete disruption when we end the class system for a period? (5, 2)
12 Veronica offering words of encouragement to competitor at Le Mans (9)
13 French banker needs safe-opener – ring Madame! (5)
14 Following current trends, serve gin this way (4, 2)
15 Conventional method of acquiring a good grip (8)
18 Sure to have some extreme ups and downs, as a vocalist (8)
20 An apple it was once simple to obtain (6)
23 Festering cut is bringing on stroke (5)
25 Ulster, maybe, for a soldier out in the cold (9)
26 A runner who goes badgering? (7)
27 See fish – Manx variety – on returning to the lake (7)
28 Through which, distressed, thy errors plead? (3, 5, 6)

Down

2 Creature of proverbial industry has eaten fruit to obtain nourishment (7)
3 This necessitates walking to work (9)
4 Tie up one of the women – take your pick (6)
5 Cloudy blue fluttering overhead in rising sun (8)
6 Lists the undesirable characters (5)
7 Signal it's not too late in the day to sack topless girl (3-4)
8 It's all to do with delivery in a dramatic performance (14)
9 Steals without being apprehended (4, 4, 4, 2)
16 Aquatic class – after I leave a cruise – act deplorably (9)
17 Scrambled egg and bread for the person in straitened circumstances (8)
19 Half-dead water bird cast up? You need to clean its feathers (7)
21 Whip will range searchingly over, for example, back (7)
22 Wattle of no use for fencing (6)

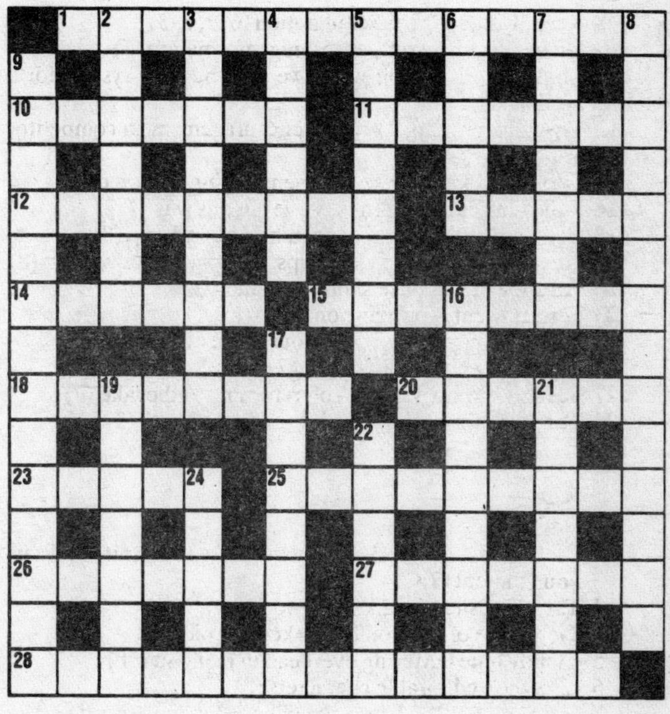

24 Said to be cunning Japanese game to get control of the board, here in Ireland (5)

17

Across

1 Scratch the game (8)
5 Hear you saw a black widow? (6)
9 A vile can ruins Spanish port (8)
10 Start to provide a good contrast (3, 3)
12 Reiterate once more, it's where the choir turns out to be – not whither (2-4)
13 Shipping company in evil clutches of islanders (8)
15 This name's not unusual but it does provoke surprise (12)
18 Men carried it off, then counter-charged (12)
23 Slovenly neglect by the brick carrier (8)
24 She is the first victim of murder (6)
26 A lager that's gone off – as sour as vinegar (6)
27 This should contain a fire (8)
28 Point to condition of the property (6)
29 One girl embraces another – it's taken to have a soothing effect (8)

Down

1 Must be rigorously precise, to cut a key (6)
2 Bird that improves conditions at Lord's? (6)
3 Fashion for hair to cover most of the chest, in tufts (7)
4 Student on assistance is made to lie (4)
6 Accommodation for two dozen singers (3-4)
7 Philosopher doing a mischief with ease, say (8)
8 Contemplates mirrors (8)
11 Home has not got much inside personal cover (7)
14 Record the activities of a lizard (7)
16 Red gases interfered with horse's training (8)
17 Unfortunate happening to find detectives taken in by a little money (8)
19 Imperative to take a worker on this month (7)
20 Oriental flower in the middle of greenery (7)
21 A stout stick is a means of defence (6)

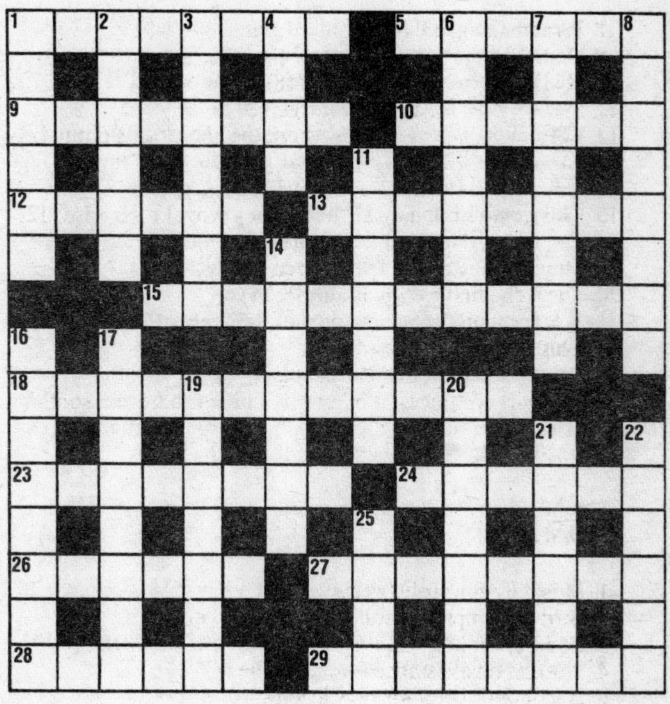

22 Attendant spirit of Egypt regrettably heading for tundra region (6)
25 Involved in twin pile-up in Greece (4)

18

Across

1 I scorn a mop – throw it out, it can be odious (10)
8 Stone in a ring given to a chum (4)
10 He can give sailor a tuna salad – but not egg (10)
11 The load we hear must take its turn (4)
13 Capital punishment for Manxman maybe for calumny (7)
15 Kiss in embrace of someone outside the church? Such indecorum! (6)
16 Make invalid ring more than once (6)
17 Fiscal analysis of a mad, droll policy? (6, 9)
18 One's state of mind when one is in a jet (6)
20 Proof corrector required for book (6)
21 Warbling on record could be off key (7)
22 Neat pair of drawers (4)
25 Salutary punishment for lad who's gone wrong, in dock (4, 6)
26 Life always the same whichever way you approach it (4)
27 The tool that should improve the pitch (6-4)

Down

2 Break bread with a foreigner (4)
3 Get by without fail (4)
4 The true interpretation of this word is not often given (6)
5 Needless in logic as the saying goes (7, 2, 6)
6 It's in here the marine ate regularly and not so often in a mess (6)
7 British Rail employee – not a waiter (5-5)
9 Going round the church notices instructions as to where one should sit (5-5)
12 Oil experts possibly manipulating their expertise to their own advantage (10)
13 It cares about being fat (7)
14 Put the lid back and get over it (7)
15 Exerting magnetic influence, they give us verbal order to take on ballast? (10)

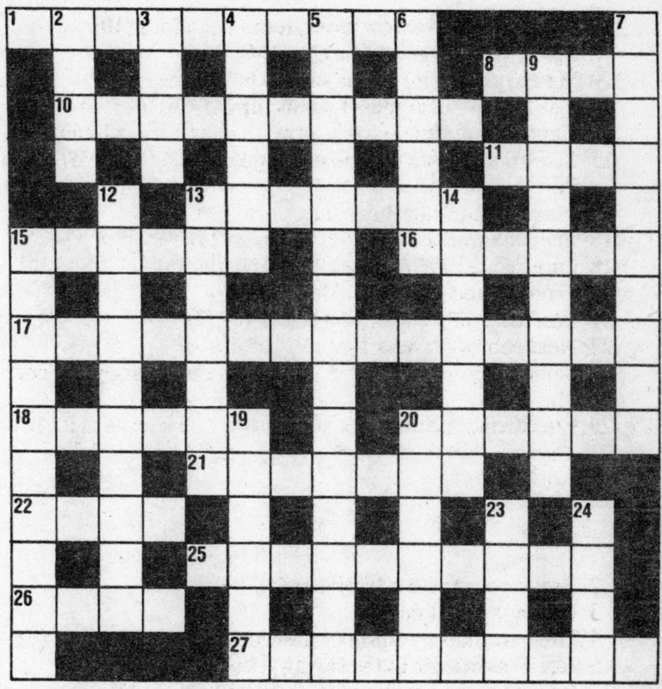

19 Those who play it aren't where they should be (6)
20 Recover, for instance, even though conditions outside are inclement (6)
23 Bark that's used in weaving (4)
24 Rabbit drawn out of a sombrero? (4)

19

Across

1 Stuff that may well be of relevance (8)
5 Reviles one who does things wrongly (6)
9 In two minds but transformed in action (8)
10 Instrumentalist provides quiet melody with reluctance (6)
12 Plates of fish (6)
13 Tea-break after Paris fashion show – one needs a breather (8)
15 Gate jammed? (6, 6)
18 The alternative course points to legal proceedings (12)
23 Put trust in book being returned, in the distant future (8)
24 Flyers in set formation may do so (6)
26 Raid medicine chest, possessing a key (6)
27 Aquatic creatures with whom a person sounds to be quite at home (8)
28 They happen to see the book the first lady's holding (6)
29 Bird and dog fit in well together (8)

Down

1 Retiring a little way, after a fashion (6)
2 This creature has a very large bill to face (6)
3 Won't be beaten in advance (7)
4 Heads or tails – you couldn't lose with this coin (4)
6 Composer named in libel action (7)
7 Looping the loop, perhaps, with high fliers (8)
8 Malicious people using fireworks that twist (8)
11 One Biblical country is like another one (7)
14 A doubtful quantity? (7)
16 Unusual for vipers to become so frisky (8)
17 Trade force about two thousand (8)
19 Quotation from an old treatise (7)
20 Can put up charge for salt (7)
21 A zebra loose in the stockade (6)
22 Subject of the pop-song (6)
25 I have a bash at Othello's enemy (4)

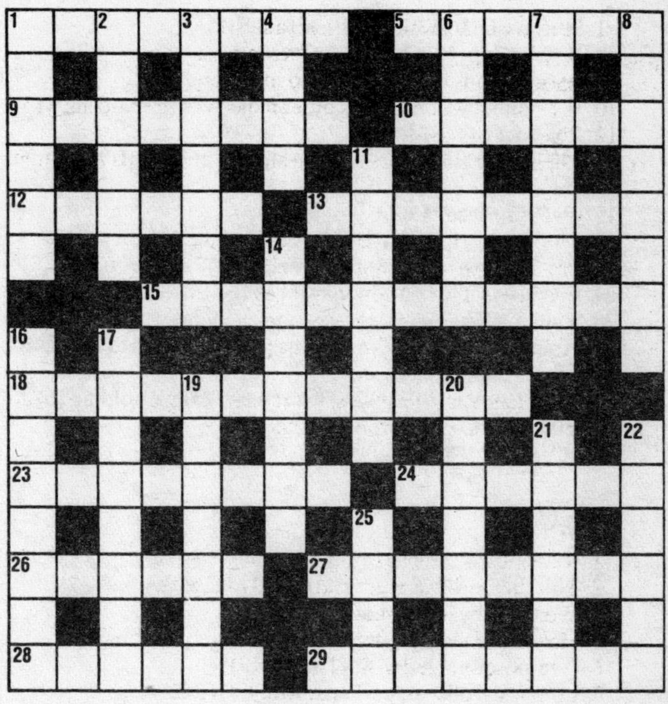

20

Across

1 New hospital got one staff appointee (11)
10 Repugnant fabrication in article (5)
11 Generate outré top career (9)
12 Port wine on tip? (9)
13 Bar measure is a troublesome topic (5)
14 Manuscript in retrospect covers the whole gamut of this political philosophy (6)
16 Skirting one stream after another coming down Etna (4-4)
18 Clop signals horrible fate hobo meets (4-4)
20 Fail to find a Latin book for the masses (6)
23 Powerful ruler once returned carrying article used in landscape gardening (2-3)
24 Simple symbol that's revered – used for healing purposes (9)
26 Star turn to go off, perhaps on horseback (9)
27 Bowls along in luxurious car (5)
28 Girl following in vehicle – it's red (11)

Down

2 Soul of an animal (5)
3 Watches the horses (7)
4 Drank and got a round ahead (6)
5 A lot of first-class timber (4, 4)
6 Growth ensues as a corm is transplanted (7)
7 Physical assault on the American fringe? (4, 2, 3, 4)
8 Unlikely foreign visitors will be turned off morning trains (8)
9 Having the ability to learn about balance sheets (13)
15 Report of Whipsnade struggle to secure animal that looks like a plant (8)
17 Aid a comb-out in the Far East (8)
19 Some bribes taint and thoroughly besmirch (7)
21 Sick and laid up, ring-leader is uncivil (3-4)
22 Like birds in the wake of the vessel (6)

20

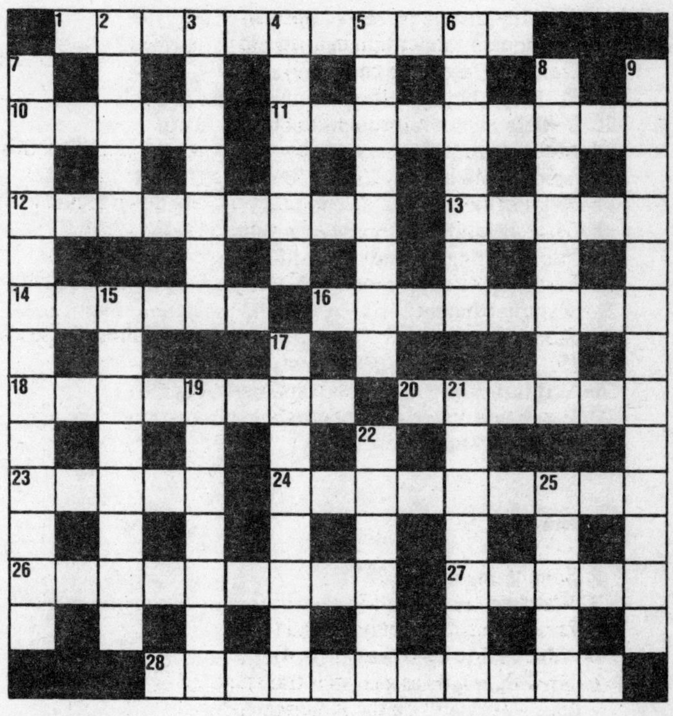

25 A boy to make one quail (5)

21

Across

1 Leading juror in favour of Eastern chap (7)
5 Transport I catch to the ministerial gathering (7)
9 Could be the pointer has gone astray (4, 3)
10 Ladies perhaps engaged drunken sailor in a row (7)
11 Endless ambition brought about this attitude, with defeat inconceivable (15)
12 Landed folk holding key to door (6)
14 Metal worker spattered enamel on the road (8)
17 Grace exhibiting glibness in translation (8)
18 Just pottering around? I'd fish! (6)
21 It's bound to be a record with shot after shot inside (10, 5)
24 Olympic competitor seen to make an attempt with pole, then sit fuming (7)
25 City which makes a bid after stylishness (7)
26 As it transpired, a reversal of many in degree (7)
27 Androgyne given direction to hold almost worthless Asian currency (7)

Down

1 Completing the trip? (7)
2 Thatched, maybe, since reed is used in its construction (9)
3 Two mothers joined the lady (5)
4 Wipe out information sent up before tea-break (6)
5 Single-minded individual? (8)
6 Beer's run out? That's the limit! (6, 3)
7 Row to North European river (5)
8 Apprehend after the initial crime (7)
13 Replacing two hoops beneath what is left (9)
15 Might take a couple to get spliced? (9)
16 Curtained off, I dropped out of box (8)
17 Conveyance for alpine trip from Birkenhead (7)
19 Yellow route diversion around Slough (7)
20 Brave the gangster (6)
22 Bracing air made one put on a little weight (5)

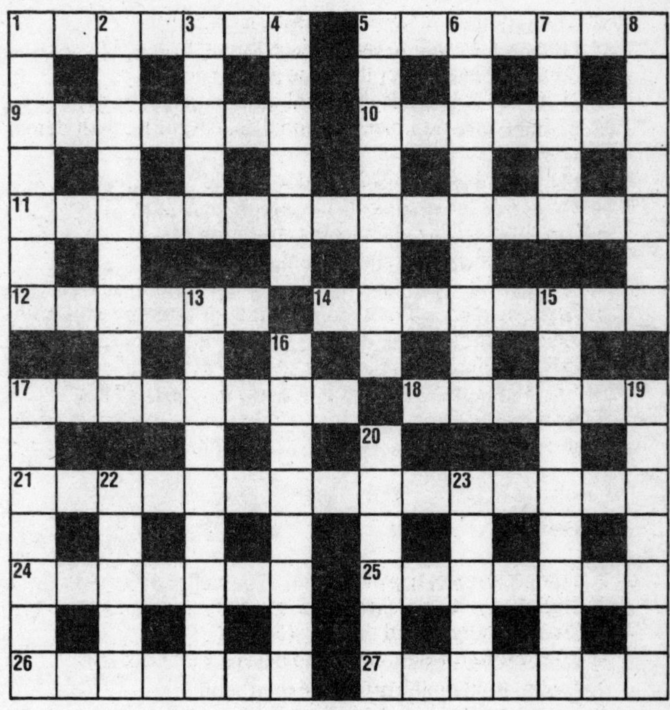

23 Cover story – I bail out (5)

22

Across

1 State it's an unwelcome beetle (8)
5 What the vendor wants, for turning in a mine? (6)
9 Rat-bites damaged the ecclesiastic gear (8)
10 Prison at an end? Must arouse comment! (4, 2)
12 Former love has nervous affliction – alluring in a bizarre way (6)
13 Caribbean isles from which we drop in explosives (8)
15 Cowardly to criticize the bunting displayed (6-6)
18 The classroom whip-round for him? (12)
23 Flies hill-dweller to the big game (3-5)
24 A sedate character, we hear, took up temporary residence (6)
26 Mr Weller and the whole company travelling west – on these mounts? (6)
27 Work abandoned for his lady love, maybe (8)
28 Sickening, after being set free (6)
29 Recalled a brief metaphor said to define a toothy gap (8)

Down

1 Has horse and trap but set out to get a fly (6)
2 Bacon with fat on it (6)
3 Rigging, a sailor must be up to the mark (7)
4 Collect one's wages with a minor rise (4)
6 Plump for a building like the Pantheon (7)
7 Lit by electricity or gas (8)
8 Try paste for the wall hanging (8)
11 The skill needed to tackle power failure aboard (7)
14 My holding on to Islamic name ensures financial support (7)
16 Fish, if badly cooked, could bring on collapse (8)
17 Insect – mite perhaps – eats half a book (5, 3)
19 Work on paper out East (7)
20 Passages introduced into books (7)
21 The primate's expression of amused surprise (3-3)

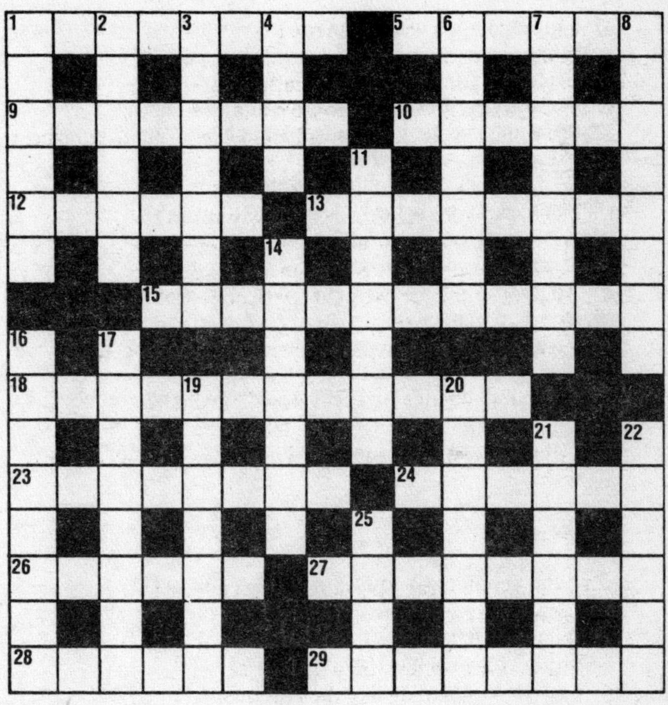

22 Port does turn out to come from South Africa (6)
25 A Nigerian uprising headed by German, in the desert (4)

23

Across

1 Figures shaped using bars in the gym and overhead weights (14)
10 Emerging from the arena without a cheer (7)
11 Double bearing flower without – or within (7)
12 By which and for which men were press-ganged (4, 5)
13 Bore before silver is inlaid (5)
14 Six-footer has joined the faction (6)
15 Fits back at angle fairly difficult to adjust (8)
18 When delivered at Lord's, is medical attention called for? (3-5)
20 All go touring around Belgium then around the world (6)
23 Reached maturity last year? (5)
25 River and wood, a local attraction (4-5)
26 The lay I rendered badly is a minor gem (7)
27 Horse moved quickly back inside to get to where the feed is kept (7)
28 Tried in court on failure of second presentation (14)

Down

2 A liar is holding a couple of articles on top (7)
3 Using this ingenious stratagem, raw beginner appears as a skilled craftsman (9)
4 Frolic around a Northern town (6)
5 Leaves, bound for the diva's study (8)
6 The key to sexual attachment is a handy sheath (5)
7 Is a gas a possible cause of that stabbing pain? (7)
8 For periods of relaxation in the sun, adder lies cushioned on leaves (6, 8)
9 Jumper the king is holding for the window cleaner (7, 7)
16 At top rate, no more room second row from the end (4, 5)
17 Diagnose trouble here in South America (3, 5)
19 String held by our friend over the water to get fish (7)
21 Swagger, getting congratulations about the present (7)
22 This palm can be plaited to make two rugs (3-3)

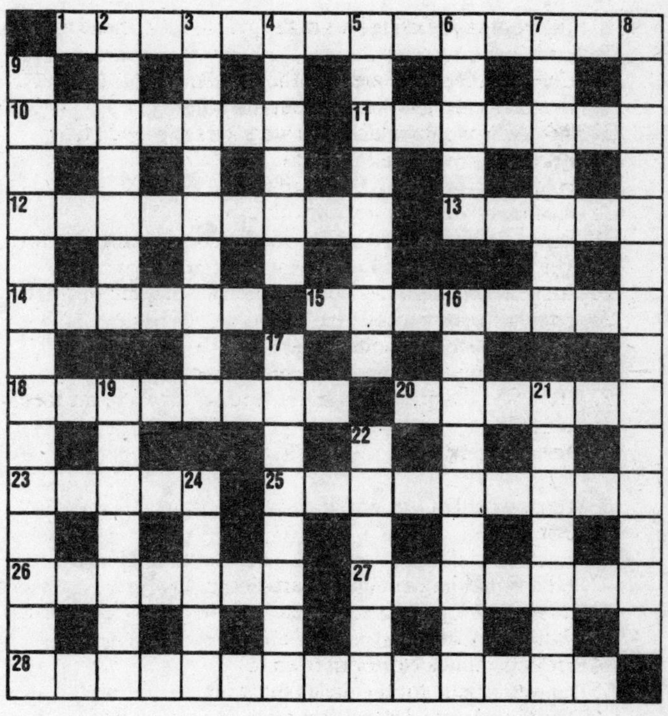

24 Torsion found in play of pontoon (5)

24

Across

4 Flier going beneath the pier (8)
8 A mere quarter-pint – that is very little for a sportsman (6)
9 In favour of certain words – they're in The Bible (8)
10 Abandoned by the Spanish in credit failure (8)
11 Those who were once in the pink expire (6)
12 Girl with a sore throat (8)
13 Rich source of wealth bemused Congo lad (8)
16 Blind man? (8)
19 Complaint making a cut only partly necessary (8)
21 I get the green stuff in return for African currency (6)
23 Idleness indeed (8)
24 A dog's life for natives here? (8)
25 Fifty-one precisely uniform (6)
26 Attempts air passage to river and south (8)

Down

1 Weapon held in a firmer, if desperate, way (7)
2 Neat substitute (9)
3 Match official indisposed – replacement called for (6)
4 Pen a signature as shakily as those in kindergarten class? Far from it! (15)
5 A lovable disposition gets the highest rating (5,3)
6 Pale echo of a doctor? (5)
7 Deliberately hurt – seemed to have a head injury (7)
14 Impersonal end in view (9)
15 Trendy relative set out to be threatening (8)
17 Men eat a pie in spring (7)
18 Bring back the cat, Tory snarled? Such intolerance! (7)
20 Alternative coadjutor has spoken (6)
22 Acknowledge that, at present, junction must be reached by motorway (5)

25

Across

1 Are thespians wary about being in a predicament of his making? (10)
6 Palm with a strong main root (4)
9 Gramophone needles in part responsible for the nasty little scratches (5)
10 Call for explanation of cryptic clue one found on a certain day in the month (9)
12 Maddened, smote scholars? (13)
14 Figure conscious – model Maureen to a 't'! (8)
15 Plane from South African state carrying political leader back (6)
17 Literary figure has to ride storm (6)
19 Extra canvas called for by novelist on the river (8)
21 Len and Peter moved out – necessary for this work to go ahead? (13)
24 Wrong to enter previous charge as blackmail (9)
25 Select type (5)
26 The result could be a win by a head (4)
27 Locked up naughty sister inside, for keeping on so! (10)

Down

1 No longer tense (4)
2 Lays out aggregate for the plant (7)
3 Oh, wherever 'tis dispersed! (13)
4 They make way for other craft (3-5)
5 Straw through which to take a pull at mineral just opened (5)
7 Red wine is brought after the meal in this catering establishment (3-4)
8 Sally – good-natured – has pound note specificially placed in butler's preserve (10)
11 The quality beyond explanation this clue must not possess (13)
13 Close attention intended, say, as a compliment (10)

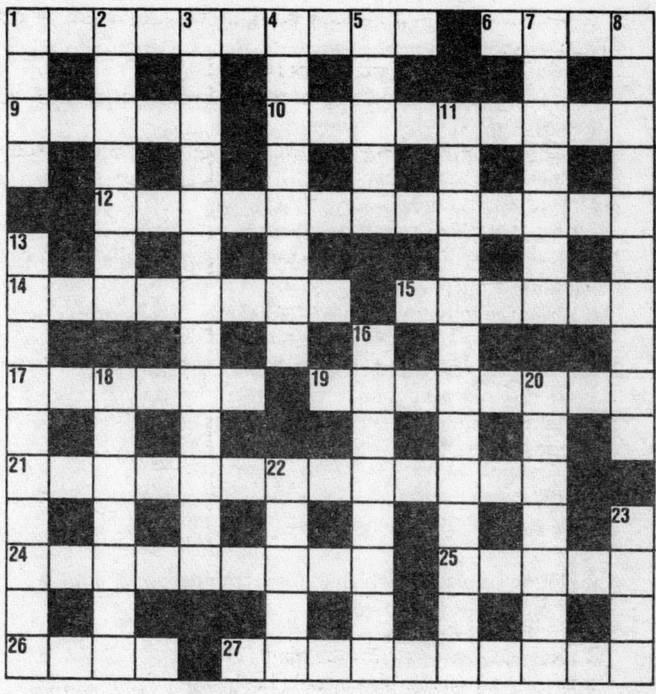

16 Pins of grog excite furtive approaches when Oddfellow goes away (8)
18 Composes fashionable ditties, dropping one note in the scale (7)
20 This window is too big for the room (7)
22 Look, then cross against the flow (5)
23 Give utterance at the opening (4)

26

Across

1 Brief study in unprofessional setting (7)
5 A temporary stoppage through amber changing to green (7)
9 Superior tropical head-gear? An ideal description (7)
10 Rather too much for an explosive train (7)
11 Go down! From penthouse to basement (10, 5)
12 Pen has an obstruction? A wire probe is what you need (6)
14 Old overcoat fits the youngest son (8)
17 Bird jumping the lights? (8)
18 Long-suffering man beheaded with the Queen on becoming king (6)
21 Happy chat the rule – with Mephisto and his ilk proscribed? (5, 1, 5, 4)
24 Entrance obstructed by much-used luggage (7)
25 Theatre row all booked, we hear – rather sad (7)
26 Tainted with guilt, is Dante reforming? (7)
27 Gun-man at the Olympics? (7)

Down

1 Hallowed place in which to dispel our despondency (7)
2 The pupils turned in (5-4)
3 Uplifting article I have found unaffected (5)
4 Preserve the name of the country (6)
5 River engulfing prince and king calls for a stretcher (8)
6 Ecclesiastic's work manual? (4, 2, 3)
7 Well-padded canon (5)
8 Go too far above the ladder? (7)
13 Tear in net – replace in hold (9)
15 A big vegetable and plump, for a pea (9)
16 A vehicle was in front but gave way (8)
17 To make room for grazing here, tree-growth must be pruned (7)
19 Around around around a pound? Get knotted! (7)
20 After I get in bed we two are becoming one (6)

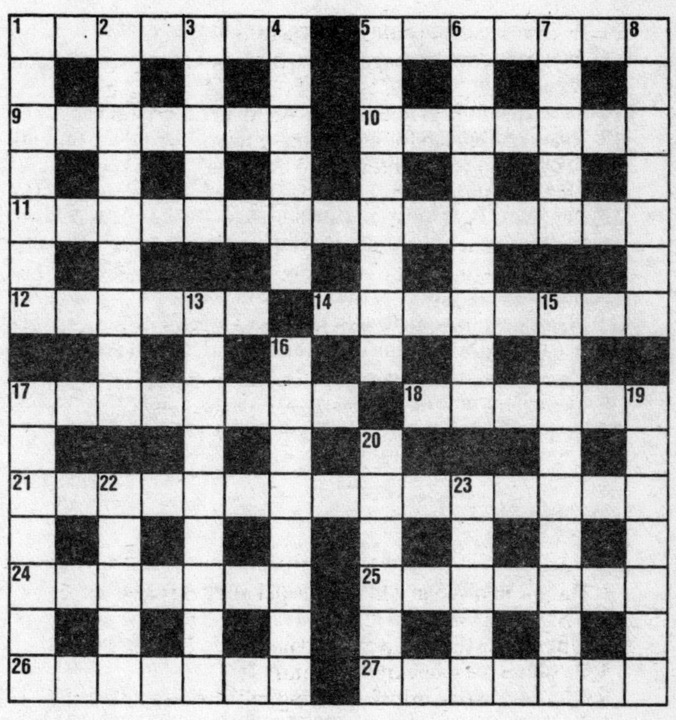

22 Evil landlord's abode (5)
23 Caught inside unfortunately going up a ladder (5)

27

Across

1 A pleasing act deserving an encore, they say (4, 4)
5 Brave couplet? (6)
9 Press for a reduction (8)
10 Forge a union with a lady novelist (6)
12 The question about the document I put in is not something to be taken seriously (6)
13 Outcome of getting one's wires twisted? (8)
15 On arrest I get awkward questions requiring answers (12)
18 Large drinks of various types bringing four people to court (5, 7)
23 Suppressing report of murder? (8)
24 Hamper is to be placed at the back (6)
26 Measures for heading off birds that eat the seed (6)
27 Queen made to thresh grain (8)
28 I tango uninhibitedly as a gypsy (6)
29 A guard appearing in battle gear (8)

Down

1 Party held in clothing warehouse (6)
2 Lady's slipper in which a creature took refuge (6)
3 The initial cause of capital crime (7)
4 The others in the bar (4)
6 Taking average time (7)
7 Hard-headed restructuring needed of bad route (8)
8 Talk with many about a specific metric construction (8)
11 A tiny bug – anxious comber has caught one (7)
14 Changed one's attitude and set the problem again (7)
16 Second brewing of tea is first rate (8)
17 Complexities need some left out, then it's clear nothing is left out (8)
19 Where it's dark and gloomy and generally at the beginning one gets beaten up? (7)
20 Left without sun but survived (7)
21 Notice something wrong in the recommendation (6)

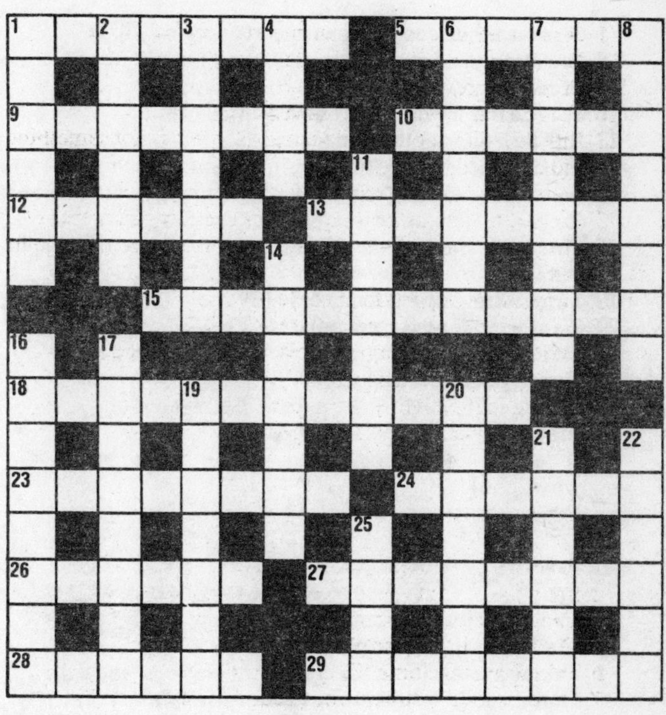

22 Caught river fish in them? (6)
25 Game sanctuary includes this flat sort of land (4)

28

Across

1 Circus animal leading front part of another (10)
8 In church an additional message has point (4)
10 Let an associate know off the record (10)
11 Such coarse food – wave the dish away (4)
13 Jute thrown over the sign (7)
15 Encountered in Opie manuscript of nursery rhymes (6)
16 Earthquake causing city to slide back to banks of the Tiber (6)
17 Manifestly showing the wicked creature savaged live rat in pen (15)
18 Twin sisters content to contend (6)
20 It's erected for the reception (6)
21 Go here to get the better of disease? (7)
22 Pluck from the sand (4)
25 Render ineffective all the patient took orally? (10)
26 Leaders of the pack (4)
27 Unloaders discovering first mate dead, buried among the provisions (10)

Down

2 I made a call in the same place, but only briefly (4)
3 Swell advertising gimmick! (4)
4 The large chest in the sanctum must block out the light (6)
5 Fruitless to go to this area of South Africa? (6, 4, 5)
6 Volunteer to make two points tally (6)
7 Product of the Queen's mint (10)
9 People get confused in Asia and under par, it's a disorder affecting the memory (10)
12 Granting this by letter? (10)
13 Retiring folk don't stay in it (7)
14 Apprentice journeyman? (7)
15 A piece of good fortune, they say, finding this food container (7-3)
19 Game you'd do wrong to catch up with (6)

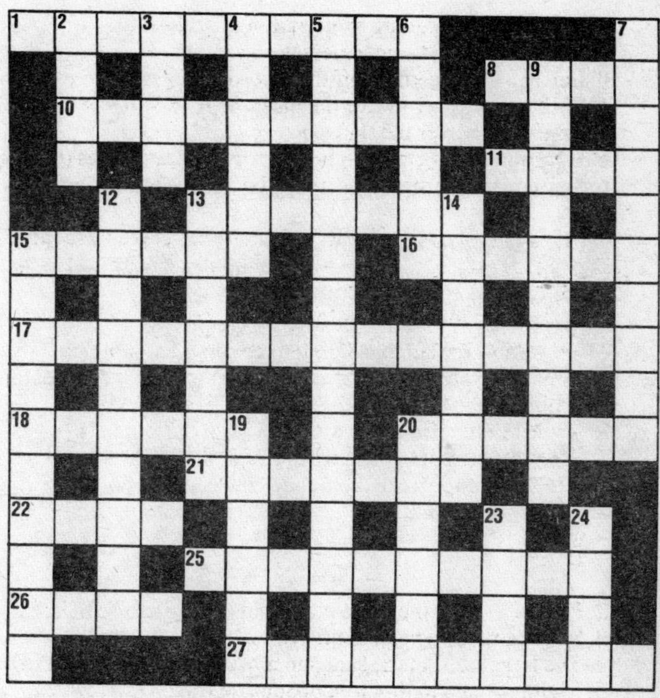

20 Recommend about five different ideas (6)
23 Member of the family with nothing on, decorating the wall (4)
24 Nothing better than a thousand, before (4)

29

Across

1 Appointments made to boards with awful predictiveness (4-10)
10 Boy finding river carp eating smaller fish (7)
11 Points to bird with the French name (7)
12 Italian mineral found to the south, a location that's a sun-trap (9)
13 Gadaffi's people in distressed state having lost an old crone (5)
14 Trendy way to attack (6)
15 Carved from stone, it's seen to wobble when moved (4-4)
18 Bloomer of the madder sort (8)
20 Sophy's turn for the holy water sprinkler (6)
23 Vegetable mould that's unfit to be served at table (5)
25 Long distance runner in a fury appears a truly formidable woman (9)
26 Type of relief for those with a disability (7)
27 Reduce the length of a crossing over the water (7)
28 He's here and attains, somehow, the goal – to hold on to the trophy (6, 3, 5)

Down

2 The tooth is gold, crowned in carbon (7)
3 Fancy having to provide every little detail (9)
4 Ursula starting to diet drastically yet needing some inner fortification (6)
5 Type of key that could be hidden in the cupboard? (8)
6 Temporal fruits (5)
7 Remarkable lack of furniture (7)
8 His plan needs to change, to accommodate the animals (8, 6)
9 Breathing with difficulty going under bridge? It gets one in deep water (8, 3, 3)
16 Management groups playing an important role in the pop group industry? (9)

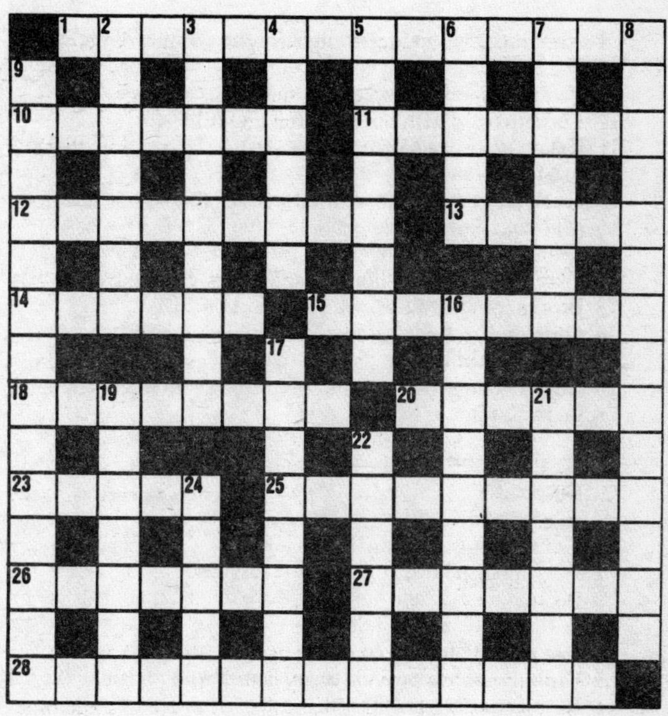

17 Light thread (8)
19 Up in arms (7)
21 Twist and twist about inside as well (7)
22 Drink up, having dined, showing judgement of wine (6)
24 See, it's holding up the conductor (5)

30

Across

4 Nonplussed at finding no boats at the quayside? (3, 2, 3)
8 For this, Basques appear in court (6)
9 Tamp even bumpy verge of road (8)
10 Turn up and queue for something to drink (8)
11 Frame brightly coloured scenes (6)
12 Frightful comedian – quite frightful! (8)
13 Stuffy, we hear, as there is no issue (8)
16 Musician playing role is single-minded (8)
19 Demonstrates staying power though not at the wicket (4-4)
21 Waif abandoned in church, companion having gone off (6)
23 Parasite that could attack the cassettes? (8)
24 Gloomy about the actors (8)
25 Ridicules the cat (6)
26 Trifles made with rum getting me nearly tiddley for a start, on the Sabbath! (8)

Down

1 Get well or get back (7)
2 Bird and fish both going for the insect (9)
3 A great many, regrettably, upset – it's the meat (6)
4 Girl tucked into fruit desserts (5, 10)
5 Not a dead bird but soon will be, perching here (4, 4)
6 Lacking confidence – on turning up, turn the light down (5)
7 Such Europeans doctored – so rape eliminated? (7)
14 In America at any rate, could be the most ignorant (9)
15 Unprepossessing insect lurking in fruit (8)
17 Turned up with a drunken driver (7)
18 Bird-dog chasing a hare (7)
20 North African tree, source of jelly that's quick to catch fire (6)
22 Race to get married and live here? (5)

30

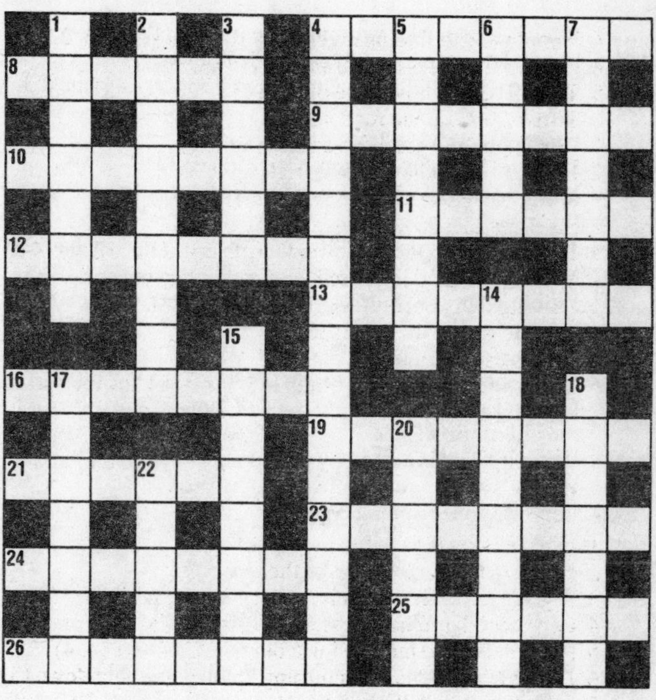

31

Across

1 Boat I've set adrift, wanting to get rid of it (7)
5 Fraudulent activities just a game? (7)
9 Having the intelligence to grasp copper ring must be harmful (7)
10 One heard to be without a glossy coat (7)
11 Surprise dash ahead of top-notch athlete (4, 4, 3, 4)
12 You need a walking stick heading for a Scottish tourist spot (6)
14 Training for young hands when they're not just hanging about (8)
17 Within a specific time a wide variety gradually ceased to survive (4, 4)
18 Supplies neckwear and bloomers (6)
21 Often sheds tears – due to this? (4-11)
24 Offhand students at the first sign of impassability retreat to the old country (7)
25 Strain it's said is caused by drink (7)
26 Frigate's stern patched up and improved (7)
27 Beryl was once a small type (7)

Down

1 Book a coach (7)
2 Waver and give up when there's trouble inside (9)
3 Standing back when a dessert is served up (5)
4 From here, a girl takes flight to the North? Not literally! (6)
5 Bearing an account (8)
6 The cockade's just too big to fit into it (6, 3)
7 Five qualifiers in the match? Vice versa (5)
8 Acolytes at court? (7)
13 Felt worried about the flyer's condition (9)
15 Gold box Rear Admiral presented to the players (9)
16 15 down again, but with girl leading them a dance (8)
17 Southern mine is impounded by Scots banker, notwithstanding (7)

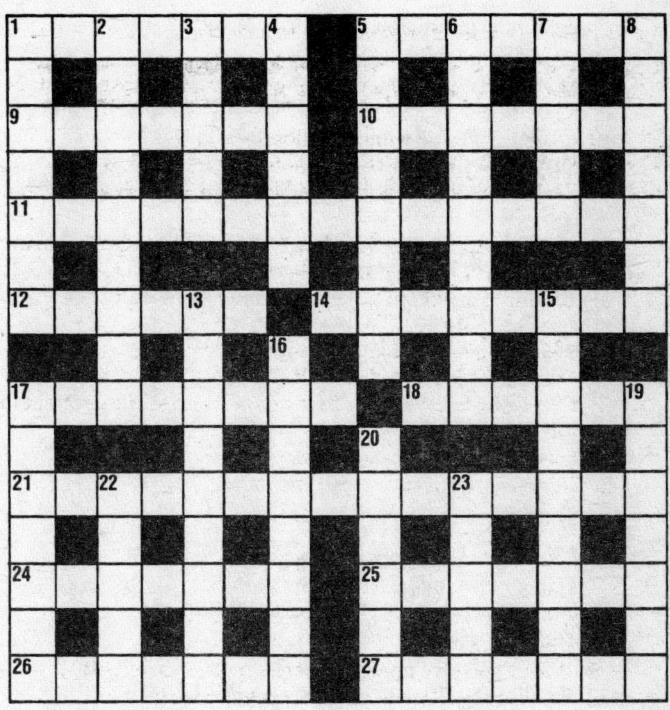

19 Puss turns tail – fearing one might do this to her, by it? (7)
20 The main thing holding the papers together? (6)
22 Mutant fleas? Entirely fictitious! (5)
23 Push needed, when you take the car out? (5)

32

Across

1 Revealing injunction to reporter (4-4)
5 Dance – or tea for two? (3-3)
9 Swan-song of the Scottish lad? (8)
10 Gives the most unfavourable assessment of the roofing (6)
12 Uncle answers and, in doing so, whitewashes (6)
13 Moving restlessly – in delirium, perhaps (8)
15 Understanding rum in a tin will have a metallic element (12)
18 The ingredients not wanted? Then some folk here may be at cross purposes (12)
23 Despondently retire, no rising again (8)
24 Assets of French art gallery (6)
26 Censor's standard? (6)
27 Swift voyager (8)
28 Get sea-sick and vomit (6)
29 Board game with directions inside the box (5-3)

Down

1 Pointing out which church requires roofing (6)
2 To get a rise, move to the south? (6)
3 Giant I thrash in very short space of time (7)
4 The sort of lie a liar produces (4)
6 Prince with one objection – fish! (7)
7 Stevenson's girl, full of spite – redhead from a Scottish isle (8)
8 Gin eases distressed recipient (8)
11 Short coat put on in the afternoon (7)
14 Horse fly problem, mounting (7)
16 Beetle a workers' group found below a cliff (8)
17 Declare the girl put on weight (8)
19 Spear fish in a river (7)
20 Wrestles with ship stuck in bulrushes (7)
21 Neat little creatures helping to move bodies (6)
22 Mourn the loss of river bird (6)

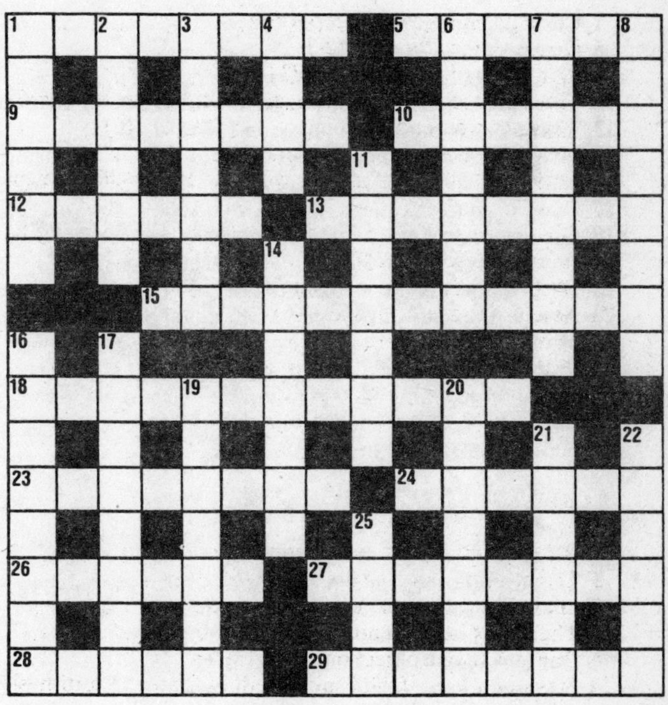

25 Showing no mercy, give her less (4)

33

Across

1 Cocktails for fellow travellers (8)
5 Services for the people (6)
9 Perform, with a lot of instruments, for playing the blues (8)
10 To be published a paper must be translated (6)
12 Time when a man of chivalry loses his head (5)
13 Two girls needed to put things on an even keel once again (9)
14 Contracted form which is flying around above Britain (12)
18 Greek found to interpret deceptive pale-face speech? (6, 6)
21 In America a sign of fall in holiday cancellations? (6, 3)
23 We hear forty of the Romans top the rest (5)
24 At one time, the first sign of illness tended to get one ostracized (6)
25 Release your grip on such a property (8)
26 Do the wrong thing and net return? It's all part of the game (6)
27 Folk add up in their heads (8)

Down

1 Taking part of the railway track (6)
2 Flooding caused by tug in waterway (6)
3 Trace bald patch – hands are often held round it (4-5)
4 Our men earn it, presumably (12)
6 A letter required by the hospital pharmacy (5)
7 It must be this medicine and no other (8)
8 Russian insect with stripes (8)
11 Urge to keep on plunging in river to reach engineer stuck at the bottom (7, 5)
15 One of nine intended, say, to create a diversion (9)
16 You are a member of this society? That's rich! (8)
17 Mixed reaction to this striking garment (8)
19 Here class distinction is the rule (6)
20 After good start boy student may finish quite happily (6)
22 Tree resin to be seen about a mile beyond the point (5)

33

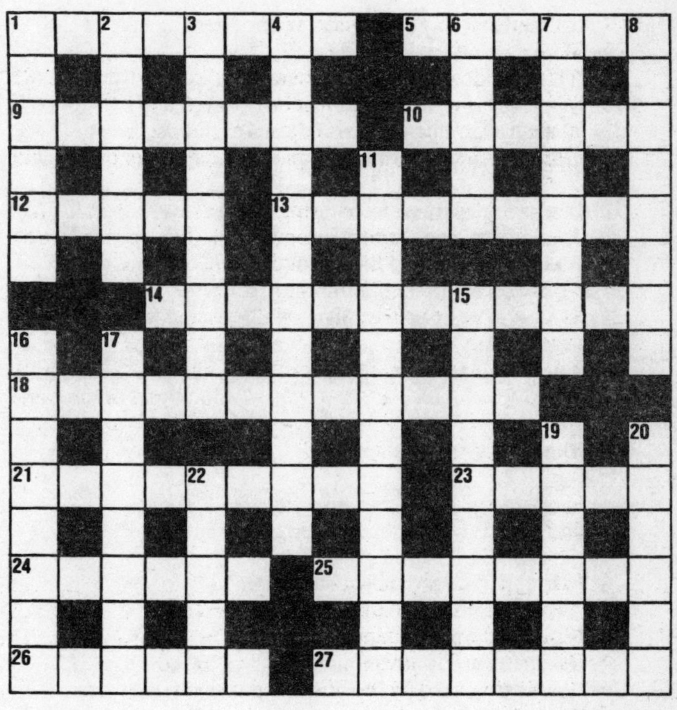

34

Across

1 At sea David's got nausea – it's not helping at all! (15)
9 Before noon, swig at a flask (7)
10 This Italian boy found bird's egg in square (7)
11 Eye-catching gadget (4)
12 Conclusive reformulation of magisterial position (4-6)
13 Banker bringing in wine relaxed regulations (7)
15 Agreeably sleepy? (7)
17 Those under the vehicle don't hold water (7)
19 Wall is a theatrical role with mimic in it (7)
20 Vehicle for transferring land (10)
22 Pool part of summer earnings (4)
25 One won't remember having it (7)
26 It's hard for first mate to tan easily (7)
27 I note ardent love – changing yet unchanging (7, 8)

Down

1 And then – devil starts heat torture? (5)
2 Stay to have something to eat and drink (9)
3 Stupid fellow is told off (4)
4 Girl takes a pudding – it's just greed (7)
5 Present in metal container is in that place (7)
6 Prime material for the plot (9)
7 Once the top is off tilts and removes the content (5)
8 Focus attention on vessel student brought into view (9)
13 Seed spilling out from box into soil (9)
14 Snooper on the prowl in outskirts of Nuneaton? He's of no significance (9)
16 I'm working on repairs for the showmen (9)
18 A swell a construction like this should contain (3-4)
19 Bundle of cards collected over a considerable time (7)
21 The occasion – midmorning at some time in the past (5)
23 Whipped, the top skimmed off and then consumed (5)
24 Not a close ring for gamblers (4)

34

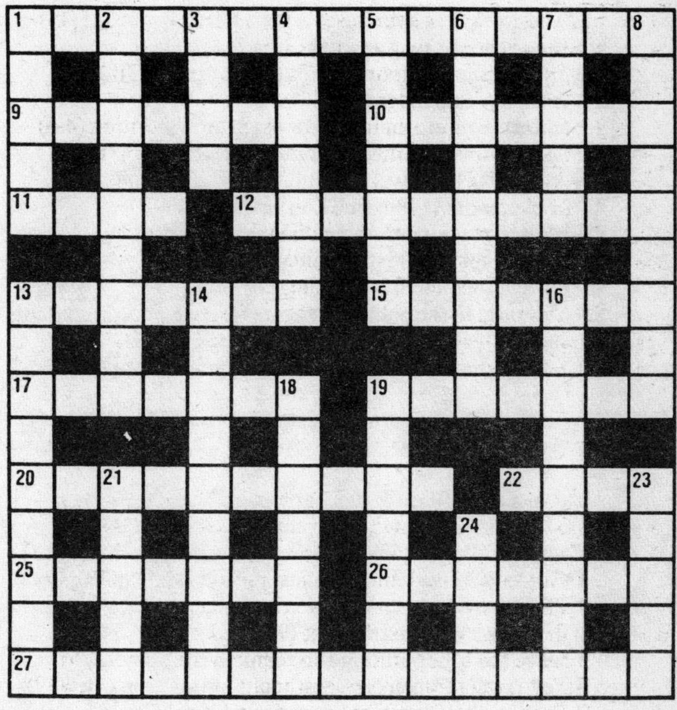

35

Across

1 Stone-worker has dropped off, we hear (7)
5 Kind of tights that may get a catch? (4-3)
9 Moody response to story about duck in difficulties (7)
10 Corruptly, I do more for money (7)
11 Sudden disruption a bolt from the blue? (9, 6)
12 Some person assaulted in popular holiday resort (6)
14 Treat EEC harshly, continuing in like fashion (2, 6)
17 Popular appeal – a march is arranged (8)
18 Fly? Parisian is repeatedly making return trip (6)
21 Happy, even though frowned on at Crufts? (3, 4, 3, 5)
24 They are inclined to show stress (7)
25 Label used in the plant to indicate when the bottle contents matured? (7)
26 Distinctive titles in new collection of verse about New York (7)
27 With its help see a North sea bird on top of lighthouse (7)

Down

1 King Merlin ousted in favour of a central government (7)
2 Disturbed Asian with a broken leg admitted an inability to feel pain (9)
3 The significance of a river in Thailand (5)
4 One put in to superintend the Church (6)
5 If tea-mug is crazed take this health precaution (8)
6 Lacking initiative, the nine to five worker? (9)
7 Girl I follow around Oman (5)
8 The others take time off before a girl appears (7)
13 Is inanity, in a word? (9)
15 Cite extra difficulty since you need to pull it out (9)
16 Hip seams torn apart by stress (8)
17 An opiate culled from secret writings in the East (7)
19 Festival to the North – or in some other direction (7)
20 Pivot on bearing coming up against vile turbulence (6)
22 Antigua not the place from which to obtain fertilizer (5)

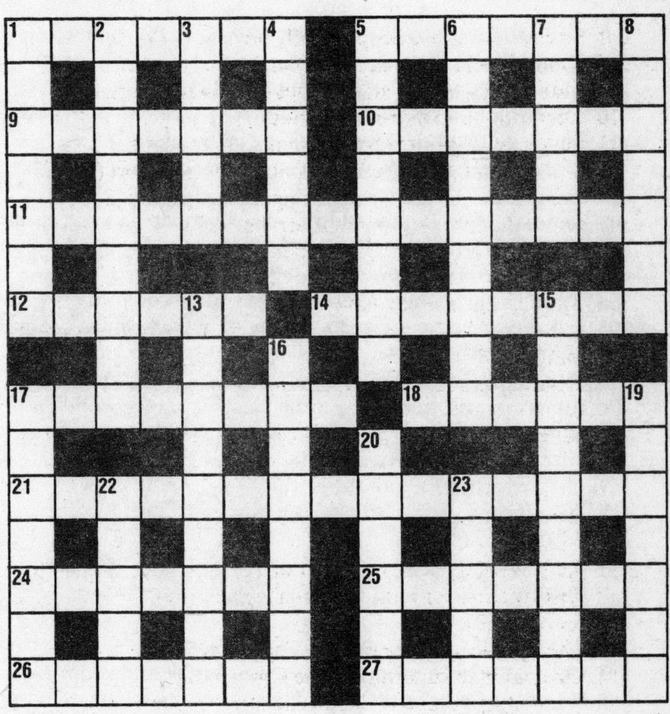

23 Saw a number ahead (5)

36

Across

1 Well-grounded course on which to have the radio commentary (5-5)
6 Mark for the second vehicle to follow (4)
9 Left right in this perhaps (5)
10 Dawn, quite fearless, captures spy in disguise (9)
12 Is absolutely certain there's a plentiful supply of water (5, 4, 4)
14 Fairy lights on bulkhead in front of banker taking a turn around deck (8)
15 When note book is not on the level (6)
17 Stenches are nothing to do with the old city quarter (6)
19 A device used by the book-maker to make firm look then ring out East (8)
21 Planting vegetables – but surely not here? (7-6)
24 Ailing operatic heroine gets financial assistance, coming to settle here (9)
25 Lift this out and there's nothing inside (5)
26 Just two articles about the novel (4)
27 The flower to linger on after a frosty spell? (10)

Down

1 Wise to relax before start of examination (4)
2 Not having been given the questions, girl pounded desk (7)
3 Princess to take vocal part in the recital – such an embarrassment! (13)
4 Food academician passes over in silence (8)
5 Shy over turning up with this creature (5)
7 It's monstrous to put me in the broken chair (7)
8 Controlling obstreperous giant with raised pistol to his head (10)
11 Team gets on well in the haulage business (5, 8)
13 Sailors given nothing in port unfortunately, for consumption (10)
16 Take action or prevent action with blocking device (8)

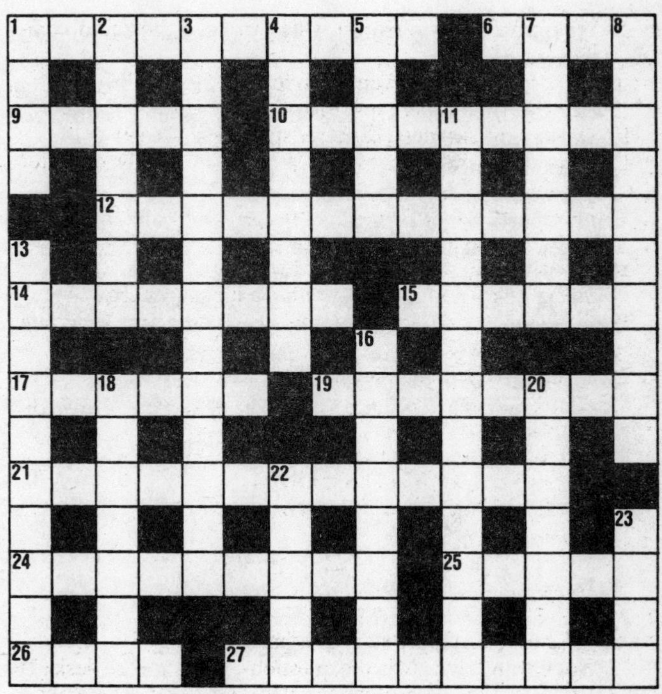

18 Seat of Empire (7)
20 Hide in hold – the Indian corn ceremony's taking place! (7)
22 Though seedy, gives a grin (5)
23 Gun carried by most engineers (4)

37

Across

1 It's calculated the Siamese perhaps returned their outdated currency (8)
5 Literally burn up the miles (6)
9 Travelling round a bend, officer's in trouble with head-dress (8)
10 Signalling of course (3-3)
12 Rows around the river in boats (6)
13 It's mortifying (8)
15 Focused attention on taking up less room (12)
18 Notice a clear roundabout – burst of speed follows (12)
23 Such thrilling play without glint of being ungracious (8)
24 Verbally mangles the sentence (6)
26 Giving longer life with some helix irradiation (6)
27 The rapid pace that's punishing (8)
28 Direction to hold silence – one must pledge one's word to it (6)
29 Glass vessel? (8)

Down

1 Two animals put back in harness (6)
2 Memorials for dogs (6)
3 Hellish conditions here making one come to a negative conclusion (7)
4 Light music at the end of soliloquy (4)
6 Greg infuriated with this Latin name for a flea (7)
7 Goes back and stands another round? (8)
8 Leaving hospital, I finish up in a semi-coma in a home abroad (8)
11 Agent lost taking medic round generator (7)
14 Two keys needed to open and lock, player found (7)
16 Charm school bearing pinpoints aristocrat (8)
17 Searching hard for means of taking out unwanted deposit (8)
19 Sprawling due to stiff gin, leaving lounge (7)

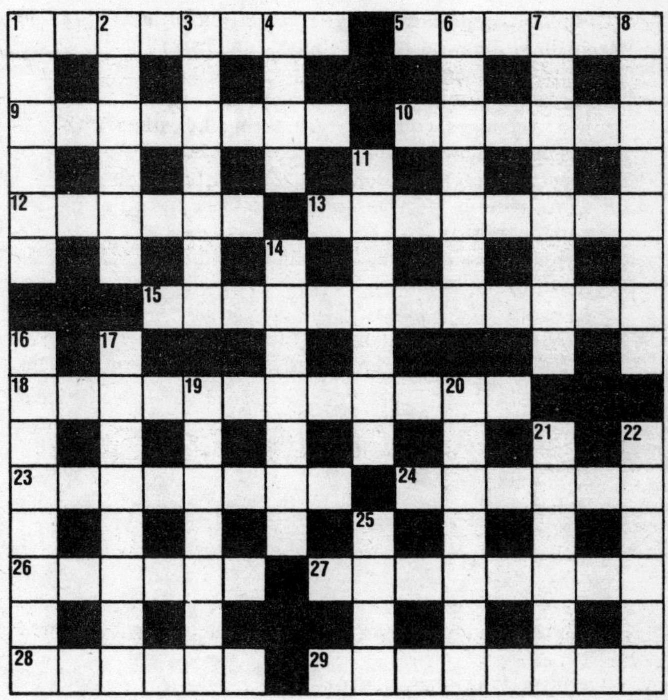

20 Novel character of gold ring around the earth (7)
21 Casting of us in close union (6)
22 Man turning up with vicar is church worker (6)
25 This tale depicts without delusions (4)

38

Across

1 A red lump starts erupting? A remedy is forthcoming (7, 7)
10 Wader follows current in underground river (7)
11 Stern-faced yet enjoying the row? (7)
12 Birds can take direction from a girl (9)
13 Mood changes, you hear, on entering the cathedral (5)
14 It's peaceful inside with fire nicely burning (6)
15 The subject, violent death – all details spelled out (8)
18 Given turkey portion, monsieur little by little applied condiment (8)
20 After a short day doing the rounds, politician has a Tibetan meal (6)
23 Late do, to be precise (5)
25 Now furled but when opened out it's fantastic (9)
26 If covered in gold and diamonds, will look just right for the opening (7)
27 Fall from a state of awareness? (4, 3)
28 The state I'm in, utterly unnerved you'll hear – wandered back, then I got bitten by a dog (14)

Down

2 Remove the door, just to madden (7)
3 Go with an upright member of the panel – it will get you in (9)
4 Off sped the detectives (6)
5 Quality of the real estate (8)
6 Notice one about to go inside and let folks know (5)
7 Unruly mob throwing trifles around – the hoydens! (7)
8 Terrifying roar . . . fled in fear . . . went this way (3, 3, 4, 4)
9 Pantomime starlets not yet out of danger? (5, 2, 3, 4)
16 Skips with girls, abroad (6, 3)
17 Watch part of skittle change direction (3-5)
19 A pragmatic view exists in the province (7)
21 So I'm of a crooked disposition, seeking the company of criminals (7)

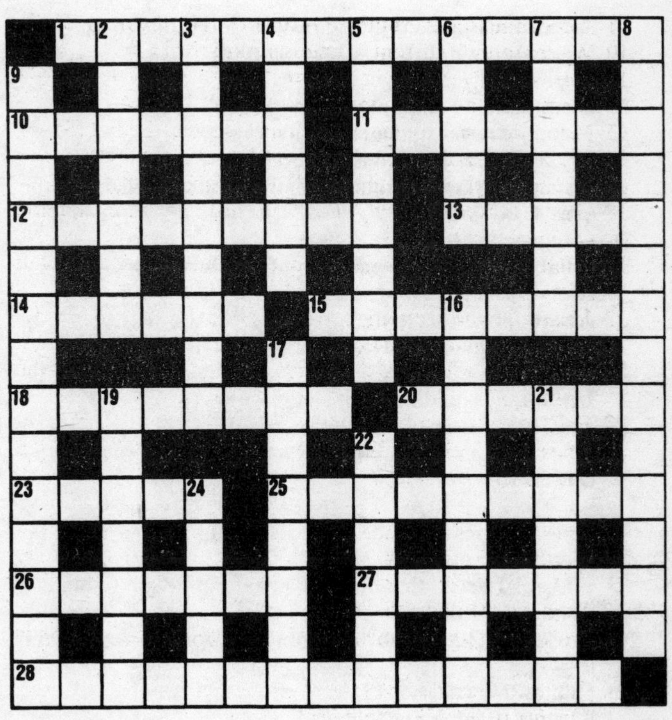

22 Shocking paths from pole to pole (6)
24 Does his best in a magisterial role (5)

39

Across

1 Scientific equipment to find river underground (4-4)
5 Light wood a mile beyond the plant (6)
9 Take and digest (8)
10 It's material to enquire after mother (6)
12 Theme of novel student read first (5)
13 Discontinues, with fall indicated (6, 3)
14 Manual workers getting the better of the regulars on the quiz show? (5-7)
18 Clay pigeon? (6, 6)
21 A habit that's sexy – semitic or otherwise (9)
23 Fancy this turning red in the morning (5)
24 Award for getting to the top of Everest? (3-3)
25 Foreigner involving us in a train smash (8)
26 Bird's-eye view? (6)
27 Lets out this holding, with all the weeds (8)

Down

1 Paths for dogs each side of the river (6)
2 Seed said to open (6)
3 Encore! The call that brought a pantomime star to fame in London (4, 5)
4 Vessel still has climb to negotiate through stormy deep (8, 4)
6 Humble tar – seasick (5)
7 Fish unsettled, being followed (8)
8 Ensure security force comes with fleet (4, 4)
11 Nurse takes doctor to decrepit hut – tramps and drifters head for it (7, 5)
15 One date's about to be changed – news briefly passed on by relation (9)
16 Sacrifice of iron hoop (8)
17 Greenhorn planted on unproductive area of rocky heights (8)
19 Most of bottled spirit a student found to be cordial (6)

20 Noontide changes (6)
22 One thousand years old? It's a facsimile! (5)

40

Across

1 Icy surface? Gravel's to be scattered (7)
5 Good example of organ restoration by dad (7)
9 Showing superior style, duck and bob around in yard (7)
10 Decapitation of knights in combat is one way of getting rid of them (7)
11 Money well spent on a stereo system? (5, 10)
12 Knotty problem for the patient without medicine (6)
14 Adores oldies – is eccentric (8)
17 Amended plans for coloured life-savers at sea (8)
18 Article first put on is the making of this handsome fellow (6)
21 Unconsidered opinion of the new publication? (5, 10)
24 Fodder by the lake (7)
25 Put into words by former word-mongers (7)
26 Footmark gives directions each side of the pond (7)
27 Fix a cap on backwards, as the pupil does (7)

Down

1 No veins, doctor, just flesh! (7)
2 Came back tied up in a pipe (9)
3 Liberal broadcast to the listener – not the common man (5)
4 Saw lady's foot, in gas explosion (6)
5 Goes ahead or returns (8)
6 Devious crossword compiler went in the van and got home again (9)
7 Escort made fun of, we hear (5)
8 Spotted holding the game up, but denies it (7)
13 Deer that's wounded shot to pieces (9)
15 The lofty thought of eminent saint (9)
16 Frank banker outmanoeuvred in stock panic (8)
17 Drunken earls engaged in very noisy forms of gambling (7)
19 Errs about employment of such cavities (7)
20 Quaker fellow meaning nothing in France and Germany (6)

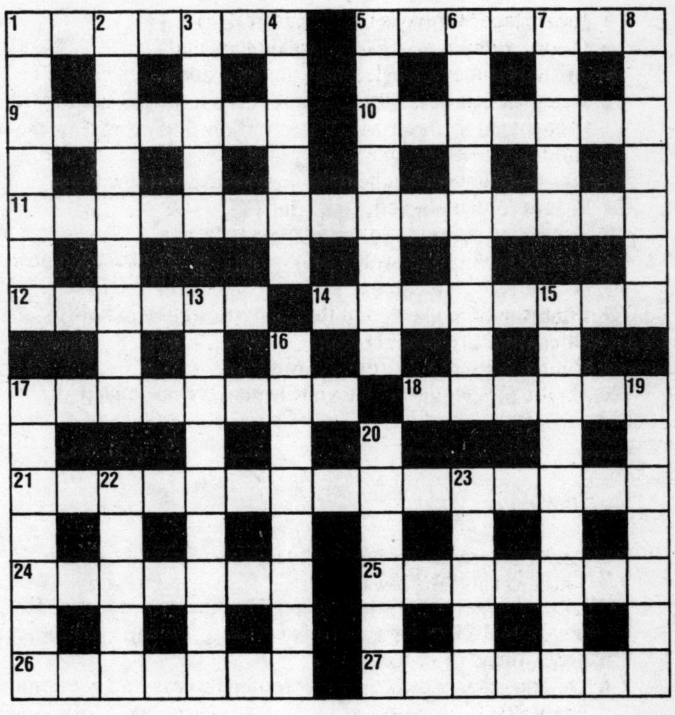

22 Not quite a member of the cloth, but on the right side (5)
23 Two points ahead of 20 down in botany this term (5)

41

Across

1 Point finger, perhaps, at clues I get recycled (11)
10 Move by river – one in particular (5)
11 Superior worker's advantage (5, 4)
12 If the publisher is, then the manuscript may be (9)
13 Union leader about to take action on finding rust in the plant (5)
14 I am so unhappy Academy rejected the line drawing (6)
16 Leaves for a meal at the golf club? (5, 3)
18 An annual presentation, possibly (4, 4)
20 Atoms uncle and I process (6)
23 Near miss? That comes of taking route diversion (5)
24 Bill brought in glass container and a purple blossom (9)
26 Doctor a marrying man? (9)
27 Vatican City to ring American state shortly, it's said (5)
28 Maybe ploughing in his profits from the stock? (11)

Down

2 Arm Eastern leader with witty riposte (5)
3 This girl eats her stew (7)
4 Routine matter of instruction (6)
5 Rapid deployment of outlay necessary for this stone worker (8)
6 Harrow tutor lost? He's gone from here! (7)
7 It's fixed to sink sewer in Britain above road, by new regulation (8-5)
8 Chum suppressing a tear – it's all to do with mum and dad (8)
9 I drag my feet around the island, a nervous complaint also making me speak this way (13)
15 Players temporarily out of action go here, leaving by coach (3-5)
17 Contriving as by magic to hoodwink one of the adjudicators? (8)

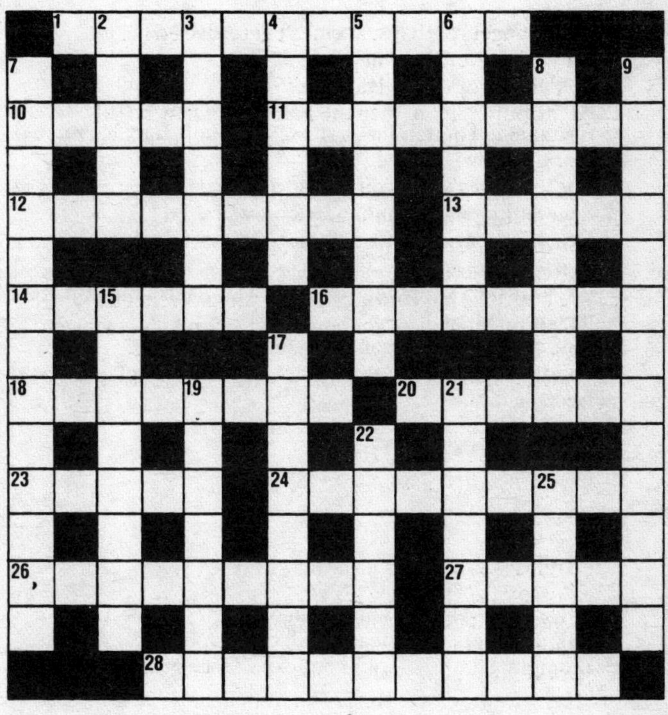

19 For starters, butchers often recommend tasty, succulent cow heels, made into soup (7)
21 One French composer. Puzzle it out (7)
22 Unfortunate outcome of that pressing engagement? (6)
25 Hospital in foreign resort – a sheltered spot (5)

42

Across

1 Scrap found by totters in part of the yard (8)
5 Bird next to fly (6)
9 Apparently failed to make out the inventory, being lethargic (8)
10 Complained of non-flier coming to an unfortunate end (6)
12 A song or two, maybe (6)
13 For this application you'll need a rubber (8)
15 Sent Smith on a scramble – eyebrows raised (12)
18 Diverting engine off track and around junction, in train snarl-up (12)
23 Caught out whipping bric-a-brac? Such uncouth behaviour! (8)
24 One out of two for example returns a pinch (6)
26 Hardly any time taken to start car, surprisingly, and it's freezing (6)
27 Heavenly article on cake decoration (8)
28 Flag officer? Not yet! (6)
29 Concern's charge for a loan (8)

Down

1 May call for pigeon holes though not for pigeons (6)
2 Take it for granted the fool will come in first (6)
3 If employed, they should not experience grinding poverty (7)
4 Feature covering only the north-west? (4)
6 Has boil, doctor, to get rid of (7)
7 Offered to nurse broken reed (8)
8 Intend to act as a medium in a short time (8)
11 Heading off conceptions immobilizes (7)
14 Cabot in voyaging collected these specimens? (7)
16 Ordered me double fibre intake – good for the skin (8)
17 Draws street car uphill to the square at top (8)
19 Crashed gear with a loud noise, in town (7)
20 On turning up gained her point but failed to get a place (7)

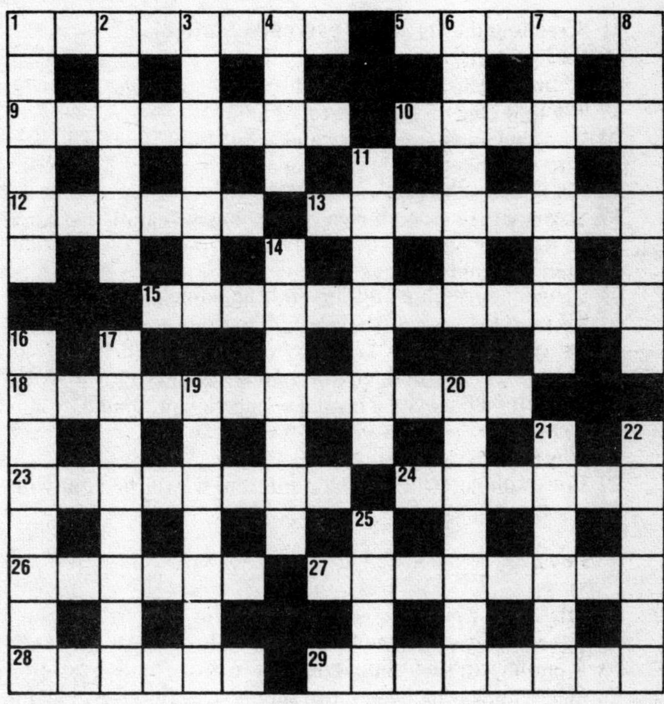

21 Urge that's said to be quite visible (6)
22 Dad takes the others out for a meal (6)
25 Article appearing soon (4)

43

Across

1 Resolved not to be irresolute (10)
8 Escorted a mother of twins (4)
10 It's mild in Spain, hence production of this fruit (10)
11 Dock, taking off first quarter of tail (4)
13 Tried me – just as I deserved (7)
15 There's money here, in Scotland (6)
16 Colour liable to run? (6)
17 Solemn, then cross, turning out to find a creature that can't be found (4, 4, 7)
18 Underground springs? (6)
20 Thirst-quenching food eaten by camel on Sahara trek (6)
21 Duck enclosure fairly insect-free but those in it lack cover (4, 3)
22 Cycle – though there's a hill coming back (4)
25 Repetition bedevilled formal application presented by him (10)
26 Clutch here? (4)
27 For example, drugs act in a different way dished out with pudding (3, 7)

Down

2 Eat out in Arab Republic of Egypt and Switzerland (4)
3 Still, the first mate has a point (4)
4 While appearing even more submissive, I object to awful reek (6)
5 Failing to resist, nevertheless? (15)
6 On top of work, it's drudgery (6)
7 Creepers twined around the marrows (10)
9 In rising scale, off-key note I sent ringing around opera-house (10)
12 Goes up and down pipes, actually losing helper in maze inside (10)
13 Engine part ought to be seen on opening drawer (7)
14 Small boy carried by physician is last across the channel (7)

15 Bringing freedom of speech? (10)
19 Global outbreak of herpes (6)
20 Location is about one mile beyond the bend (6)
23 One part of a continuous uprising (4)
24 Lines Her Majesty sent to a small relative (4)

44

Across

1 Remove soft centre to reduce bulk (7)
5 Monitoring device failure at the plant (7)
9 His enthusiasm does not encompass the simpler varieties? (7)
10 Running dogs I've dogged (7)
11 Ideal for ringing the changes in bed? (10, 5)
12 Den is about right, it's well built (6)
14 All work in a wet and sticky environment, as parachutes should do (4, 4)
17 British politician starting a quarrel at the terminal (8)
18 Is sent back by mistake to a mountainous area (6)
21 Prove one is ripe for the picking by handing over the cash? (5, 2, 3, 5)
24 Chap at extremes of endurance about to give out (7)
25 Prince requires weather report for the Spanish plains (7)
26 To play part lines call for effective props and backcloth (7)
27 Beer, it gets spilled on yard, due to drunkenness (7)

Down

1 After failing, old Bob crosses to the other side (7)
2 Travelling up lanes in Spain and Portugal (9)
3 Deportee I left in river (5)
4 Ring Berne, sort it out, then invest (6)
5 Camel train stampeded by reversing taxi (8)
6 Big IRA lad crunched a currant biscuit (9)
7 English college from the Loire (5)
8 Makes progress in a relative sense (7)
13 Remove the water – they dread being spattered (9)
15 Rodent leading us to gold chalice buried in the wood (9)
16 Facetiously depicted as close entwined in embrace of a beloved one (8)
17 Girls like boys (7)
19 Set out to attract some tips (3-4)
20 Prime object of care (6)

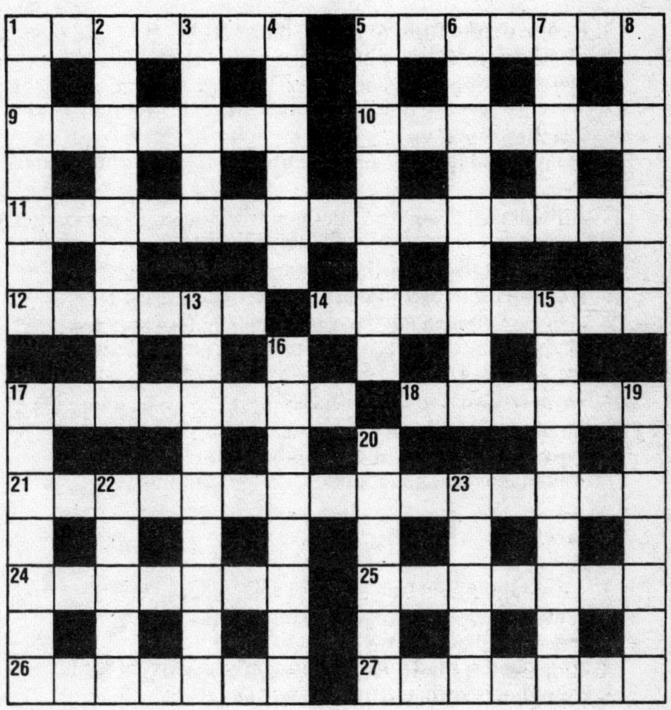

22 Circumvent bill put in the day before (5)
23 Making an effort, I get right up beside Her Majesty (5)

45

Across

1 Vessels in which one cooks hedgerow fruit (10)
6 Search all the cells (4)
9 Name understood (5)
10 Bishop staggered a little way following this journey overseas (9)
12 Sandpit scouring – East European's cleansing ritual (4, 3, 6)
14 Bottleneck in holy city, he found (8)
15 How to get your own back? Give it further consideration (6)
17 No point in partner breaking record again (6)
19 I ask chef about something on the menu (8)
21 Happy with fourteen pound pair of trousers designed for doctors? (9, 4)
24 Novel knitwear in America (3, 6)
25 Put on one's best suit (5)
26 Lyrics to start off dramatic productions (4)
27 Frank takes seat abandoned by those standing (10)

Down

1 Utilized for sport on board (4)
2 Something laid on us, cruelly, to get us moving (3, 2, 2)
3 It's ground spread out and frequently iced over (8, 5)
4 His millet is perhaps from Mexico (8)
5 Nosed into parking after bumpy ride (5)
7 Oil swirl across pane gives this milky iridescent appearance (7)
8 Plot by cleaning lady to bring order into this room (10)
11 Inconsolable and distraught, he drank beer too, endlessly (6-7)
13 Indigenous sailor with novel (10)
16 Fish we caught and gazed at, in astonishment! (4-4)
18 Leaving junction jerkily am wary of these lines (7)
20 Lust as a basis for a personal attack (7)

22 So is a fiddle as easier alternative proposition for musicians? (5)
23 Elects for new post (4)

46

Across

1 It offers several outlets for a chap if past his prime (8)
5 Usual standard a beginner carried (6)
9 A plant to sway a girl (4-4)
10 A complaint I got from a rodent (6)
12 Gaunt with love Dicky's sweet! (6)
13 Old hat for a lady to take to this instrument? (8)
15 Pass our plan for the decor (6, 6)
18 Perverse Latin masters will? (12)
23 Open jar is upset (8)
24 Take exception to the article (6)
26 Showing pressure, lives round the pub (6)
27 In favour of the leaflet, draw it out (8)
28 Furnished as appropriate in den refurbishment (6)
29 Set upon as left the quayside (8)

Down

1 Airman flying out to naval base (6)
2 Can out-manoeuvre a night flier (6)
3 Confusion caused by boisterous prank interrupting a game of cards (7)
4 Vessel's inclination to roll (4)
6 Love and caring turned out to be a vital matter (7)
7 Doctor frees the policemen (8)
8 Deposited egg in front of the coop, ready for inspection (4, 4)
11 Polite yet with brusqueness taking charge of ball (7)
14 Workers who become members of society (7)
16 Held fast but with room for me to move around (8)
17 Free rides to a minor planet (8)
19 Wagon driver has to reverse direction and find the way back (7)
20 Change of habitat for her (7)
21 Soldiers queue to pass on report (6)

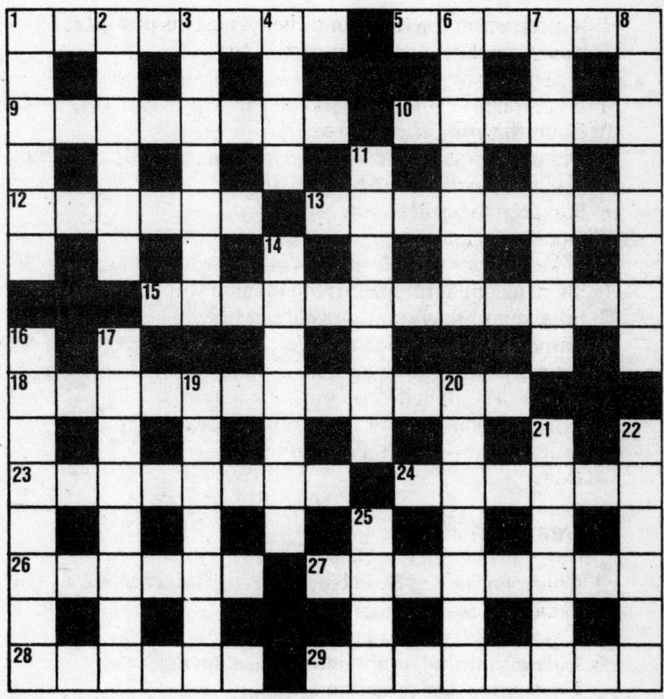

22 Declared art collection must be housed within the borders of Scotland (6)
25 Flag girl (4)

47

Across

1 Good, warm lowland put to new use, arousing most bitter resentment (4, 3, 8)
9 Provisions here for fabulous bird with ruffled grey plumage (7)
10 Joins the army after I leave (7)
11 Amphibian said to have been dragged along by a rope (4)
12 College for riflemen? (10)
13 Tin seen to buckle under strain (7)
15 Steamship may be going out to this mission (7)
17 Candle Mary carried going back to the tomb (7)
19 Filed irregular returns? He may catch you out (7)
20 The punters among us? We are advised to show them respect (3, 7)
22 Pole entering by way of special sanction (4)
25 Report I compiled – columns of it (7)
26 Someone antagonistic is a problem at work (7)
27 Guess, then, our sin. Perhaps this? (15)

Down

1 Mutton procured by soldier (5)
2 Tend to lack foresight? (4, 5)
3 Tip-top pea soup for ten (4)
4 Tide may turn, but not during the night (7)
5 Extra large slice dished out with little bone (7)
6 Adaptable you'll find me, competent to do just about everything (9)
7 After a century lost, secret is uncovered (5)
8 Ship breaker (9)
13 I am on time you hear, coming on the spur of the moment (9)
14 Unfeeling and wicked ringleader to be taken out for telling off (9)
16 Publication supporting the team is not the main item for consideration (4, 5)

47

18 Harry tried to get this place (7)
19 If so, our eccentric is a madman (7)
21 Sovereigns are held though less often seen (5)
23 Hanging a king and foreign prince (5)
24 Work for those who play (4)

48

Across

1 Spirit that's a household word (8)
5 One member of the university unable to obtain a degree? (6)
9 Telephone request that the jilted suitor might hope to get? (4, 4)
10 Fish trained, we hear, to swim backwards (6)
12 Scene of intense activity near a roundabout (5)
13 A domineering old woman, yet somehow Rita has charm (9)
14 Gets a gin sling – but when bill's first presented there's abusive language (12)
18 Domestic ties (5, 7)
21 Spin a long-playing musical recital (9)
23 Try to avoid meeting bill put in the day previously (5)
24 The wounded just start to come out – one gets hardened to it (6)
25 A base in Japan for Indian novelist (8)
26 Secured some yellow patterned cloth by this process (3-3)
27 He flashes past, but not in gear (8)

Down

1 Make-up intended to be applied to dull, roughened skin (6)
2 Primate, a man of habit, finding elegy unsupportive (6)
3 Book-keeping expert (9)
4 Law-suit about copper and alum turning up in the pile (12)
6 Foreign friend importing a tip-top violin (5)
7 Express impatience when study circle brought up the subject of coaching (8)
8 Fun-fair magnate? (3, 5)
11 A sit-down meal? Quite to the contrary and is not to be moved on this issue (8, 4)
15 Easter egg brought round, then set aside (9)
16 Battle colours (3, 5)
17 Tool needed to put together old city in the interior (8)

19 Rose to interrogate mother first (6)
20 Row me over in pursuit (6)
22 Wanting jumble – East End youth leader (5)

49

Across

1 Shawl knotted around hip leads to a form of spinal injury (8)
5 A thought proved diverting (6)
9 Complexities could become clear were some removed (8)
10 Altitude and atmosphere right for a star of first magnitude (6)
12 The clown is willing to take a part, in this case (6)
13 Shrub's new growth ideal for transplanting (8)
15 In this sporting event, after a hard climb Charles loses heart and falls out (12)
18 Prisons in which certain races may be tortured (12)
23 Welsh river bird perched on rear part of ship (8)
24 How's that for charisma? (6)
26 Like a centipede, with scales (6)
27 Dread the doctor getting needle ready for suturing (8)
28 Spectacles a help when out sniping (6)
29 No complicated choreography for these dances (3-5)

Down

1 Emotional pain felt on parting with a tool (6)
2 Strike is a mischief-maker's doing (6)
3 Free-range eggs put on display? (4, 3)
4 Narrow opening in which there's little room to turn (4)
6 I leave domicile for a change of air (7)
7 High-flier in the advertising milieu? (8)
8 Not a fair description of times long past (4, 4)
11 When training, coach's call to member of tug o' war team? (7)
14 Cite her as one not having the right views (7)
16 Can a levy, so to speak, be put on nails? (3-5)
17 Deriding gluttony (8)
19 Dish quite excellent – took a morsel (7)
20 State train (7)

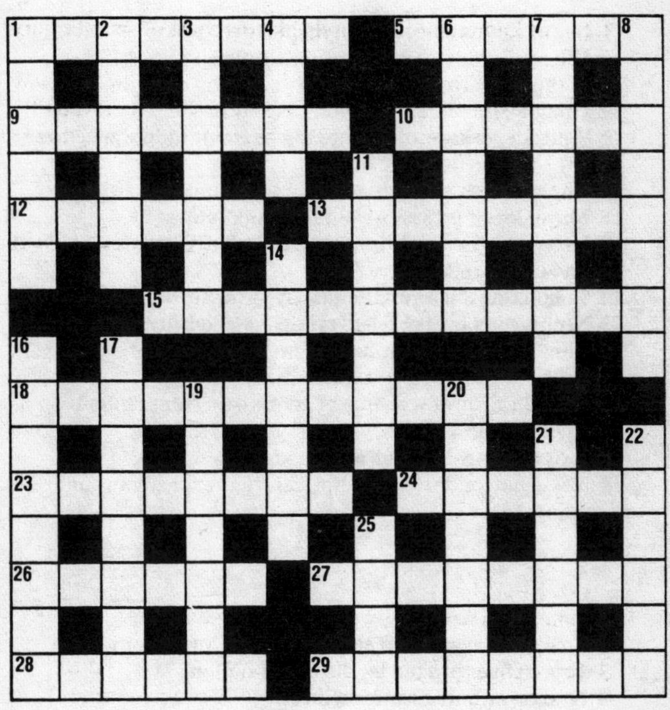

21 Workers' group providing refuge for lad thrown out by parish official (6)
22 Skates and goes flying (6)
25 Dog food (4)

50

Across

1 Groom given ring, here in the theatre (5-6)
10 She needs help carrying article, travelling West (5)
11 It's secret – by new regulation no credit is given at end of article (9)
12 Weedy, perhaps, due to being beyond the normal height (9)
13 Replacement of nut that is loose (5)
14 The colour that's supposed to shrink? (6)
16 Instrument certainly has end piece missing, confound it! (8)
18 Avoid fish and poultry (8)
20 Confection consumed in a province of Germany (6)
23 Nothing in jar I replaced? There should be wine (5)
24 Compulsion to make sweetheart kiss it – or not, perversely (9)
26 A wildly disordered state of affairs – master set about pupil at end of term (9)
27 So is a change from all that sand (5)
28 Negligent raider blown up, carrying explosive round the point (11)

Down

2 Free, for example, to climb up to this lofty position (5)
3 Stretch over broken leg – a bright notion (7)
4 Barrier with string attached (6)
5 Have confidence in foreign money accepted lately (8)
6 Listlessness observed in monkey that's off its food? (7)
7 I'm clever and sound, working out what criminals have got away with (8, 5)
8 Lending enchantment? (8)
9 Fiend set clues – trickery involved! (13)
15 The survey's no longer ancient history? (4-4)
17 Put in last place (8)
19 Initially Albert is devoured by lion – hence the hook-up (7)
21 Showing strain left take-off point (7)

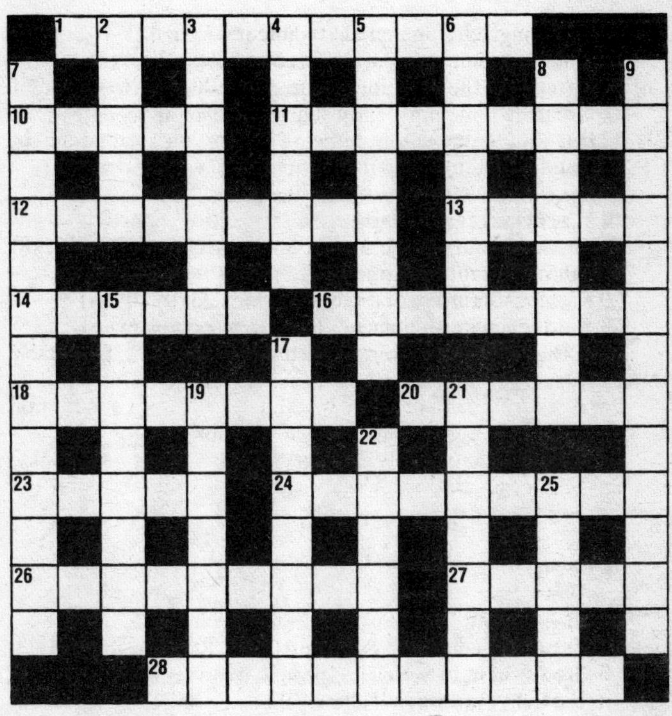

22 Frustrate the dim-sighted Scot (6)
25 Playwright Benson is unfortunately abrogating the issue (5)

51

Across

1 If retiring, take up domicile where it's warm (8)
5 Student prank in a moment becomes calamitous (6)
9 Two things the matador will need for his virtuoso leaps (8)
10 Defames some most earnest and respectable scout leaders (6)
12 Condemnation called for, so quietly leaves the podium (5)
13 Issue a setback for me before the race (9)
14 Voters making things up (12)
18 The last clothing you'd want in a gale in Gateshead with lightning that's continuous (7, 5)
21 Each lad in turn to find fare from Mexico (9)
23 Get in touch with preacher for each is missing (5)
24 In the distant past I put English behind bars (3, 3)
25 Niches get almost entirely occupied by these lively prints (8)
26 Band sailors can obtain without question (6)
27 Came to a melancholy end, they say, covered in woad (4, 4)

Down

1 The agent often taken into account (6)
2 Go off and make good (6)
3 Fiery mount scattering soil around royal sepulchre (9)
4 Red light seen when landing gear's needing to be replaced (6, 6)
6 Odd leading seaman getting up to dance (5)
7 Treading with difficulty due to the camber (8)
8 Warmth and comfort of island I head for (8)
11 Nasty rash I'd treat with phosphorus – it's the foreign food! (6, 6)
15 Ferreted out a dangerous electrical appliance (9)
16 Display sorrow and become vocal about such changes (8)
17 Risk neck, perpetrating bloomers (8)
19 Murderous waterway passing round another (6)

20 Has a follower, we hear, but does not succumb to temptation (6)

22 In boxing lesson keep to corner (5)

52

Across

1 It's extremely hot here in the plant circle (7)
5 Hard tack and bully beef? (7)
9 Hunting man's hobby (7)
10 Ringleader befuddled, the worse for wear (7)
11 Free licence for a wrestler (5, 2, 5, 3)
12 Warbler I chased from north of the woods (6)
14 Biters, these canine neighbours (8)
17 Rash the child and I got travelling in the East (8)
18 Take away support for a member (6)
21 Dreams of rooks, wheeling? (7, 2, 3, 3)
24 Lifting equipment holds fish by end of tail (3-4)
25 Noise or disturbance can be wearing (7)
26 Some day may be employed as a barker (7)
27 Great distress when it is fired (4-3)

Down

1 Devilish deeds, strikes! (7)
2 Initial error made by the fielder (5, 4)
3 Uneven part of the links (5)
4 One who sees things from this angle can be hard to convince (6)
5 Put on a brave face (3, 5)
6 Editing material for socialist movement (9)
7 Courtly presentation of pickled cauliflower head (5)
8 Conclusions drawn from words such as 'amen' (7)
13 Rarely lit fuse set off arsenal (9)
15 Working on tape rig makes a change (9)
16 Encourages a boy to get something to eat (3, 5)
17 Something nightmarish in the animal bearing down on us (7)
19 Bullies try maltreating the workers (7)
20 Requisition tinned stew (6)
22 Lily headed south for this old English town (5)
23 Bend a pipe (5)

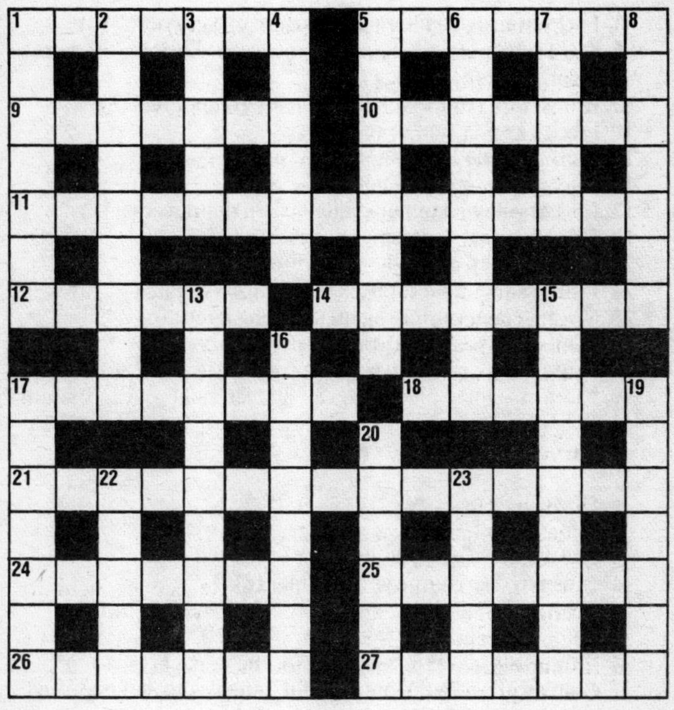

53

Across

1 Girl suffering confinement because of this youth? (8)
5 Time when Harris's Uncle went round backing the horse sure to lose (6)
9 Gangs capturing oil installation are freebooters (8)
10 Deck's knotty timber (6)
12 Member dined with the ambassador (6)
13 Receptacle for the small fish I catch (8)
15 Masters may be impersonated when out of form (12)
18 Unable to hatch perspicacious ideas? (5-7)
23 Think how to make the duck fly up (8)
24 Distress signal set off by castaway (6)
26 Team in anger rejecting invigorating liquor (6)
27 A blow for someone bringing in the harvest (8)
28 Santa likely, initially, to move cautiously on it? (6)
29 From this lofty place you can almost make out the South Pole (8)

Down

1 Physician with ill-humour's easily moved (6)
2 Mean to overcharge youth leader (6)
3 With additional information provided, modify the book (7)
4 Knot that is undone (4)
6 Terrorist's initial justification for the crime (7)
7 Ship's officer goes out in rain squall – to get thorough soaking in it (8)
8 By far and away the most unlikely thing to be brought up to me in the interval (8)
11 Save the girl – a local worker (7)
14 Speech might indicate where one's home is (7)
16 Speed makes for security (8)
17 Had trouble over points I have briefly found sticky (8)
19 This decoration may have a hook but it does not fit the eye (7)
20 Philosopher's calculations are upset (7)

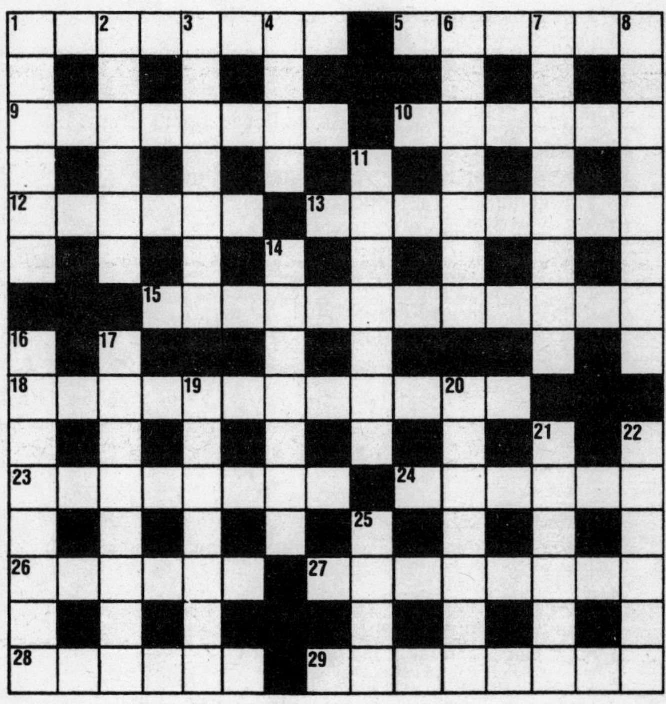

21 But would there be room in it for so many potatoes? (6)
22 Disclose Union leader takes prawn cocktail (6)
25 Exceptionally good headlight (4)

54

Across

1 Joke sent him out of court – to jail (10)
6 Forbidding this endless dirt (4)
9 Drink the horse needed (5)
10 A melting performance (9)
12 Defended territories – reassembling troops at Crete (13)
14 Tilting object is a wheat cracker (8)
15 Rasher cut up and offered around by him (6)
17 This cult flourishing 'mid sun? (6)
19 Smelling of this – react fast! (8)
21 Foundrymen making patent remarks (7-6)
24 No tied house in Yeats' isle? (9)
25 Indication of low interest rate (5)
26 Doesn't stay for functions (4)
27 Extricates first mate squeezed right inside swamp vegetation (5, 5)

Down

1 Father holding up this case (4)
2 One of the things it's fun to knock – can't be wrong, they say (7)
3 Emerging from the classrooms? (13)
4 Damage to measure inside the tower (8)
5 Nine players and not one on time! (5)
7 Revel in making foreign monarchy rest uneasily (7)
8 Stratagem I deployed to get to the provost (10)
11 A natural tremor – though with heart flutters some folk get a couple of doctors around (5, 8)
13 Claiming ownership of certain birds, exchanging about a third of number (4-6)
16 Mountain dwellers seen out around the enclosure (8)
18 By the river cast net, in time finding it's relaxing (7)
20 Fundamental nature of sentences New Testament omitted (7)
22 Tend to take Union's direction (5)

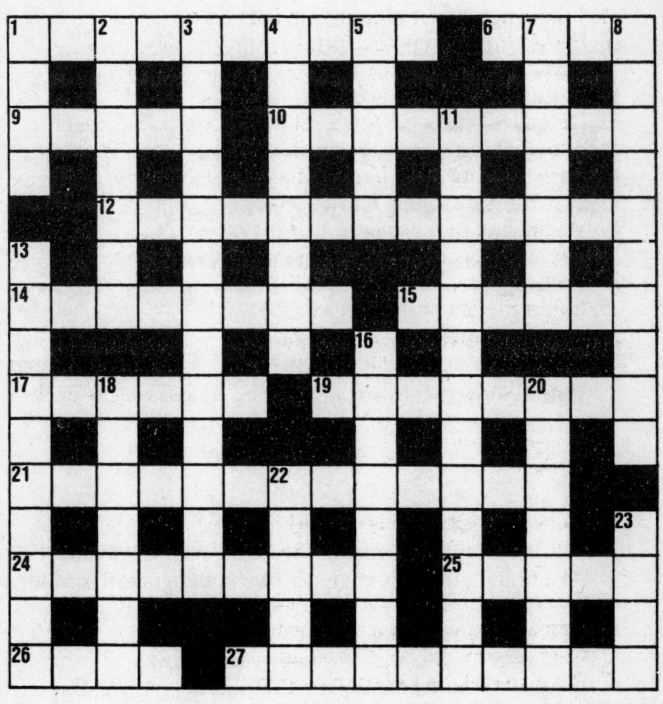

23 Goes into competition, getting half a dozen points (4)

55

Across

1 Dismissals left and right (8, 6)
10 Instrument to obtain one cubic centimetre used in game (7)
11 Freebooter gets a little cold – strong ale's called for (7)
12 Bird goes for bulb or insect (9)
13 An alert bird-woman (5)
14 It's used to secure mince pie in container (3-3)
15 Painter making girl and I go in backwards (8)
18 Provided the solution when weeds ran riot (8)
20 Or puts stew in the vegetable dish? (6)
23 Poet returning to isolated spot abroad (5)
25 See zebra taking trip East by air moving along the coast (3-6)
26 Fairly big and has girl staggering (7)
27 Food for a fellow, at one (7)
28 Military movement proved accurate in assessment of the act (5, 5, 4)

Down

2 A county cricketer sure to be ordered off – blast him! (7)
3 Fish eating bird on foreign isle? Something more formidable! (9)
4 I thus resist equal pressure (6)
5 Good start to river trip – getting plastered (8)
6 Judges deserter from mid-West (5)
7 Restraint therefore needed, covering BMA turn-out (7)
8 A jumper will do so it seems winter's nearly over (6, 2, 3, 3)
9 Advertising salesman from Mars, maybe? (5, 9)
16 Bring an insect into the country? That may be a serious matter (9)
17 Blames him when student gets lost, travelling with her (8)
19 Risk gun misfiring, to gain this trophy? (4, 3)
21 Ring writer before broadcast – it's alfresco (4, 3)
22 Munch a pie – Chinese (6)
24 Dance with a Dickensian character (5)

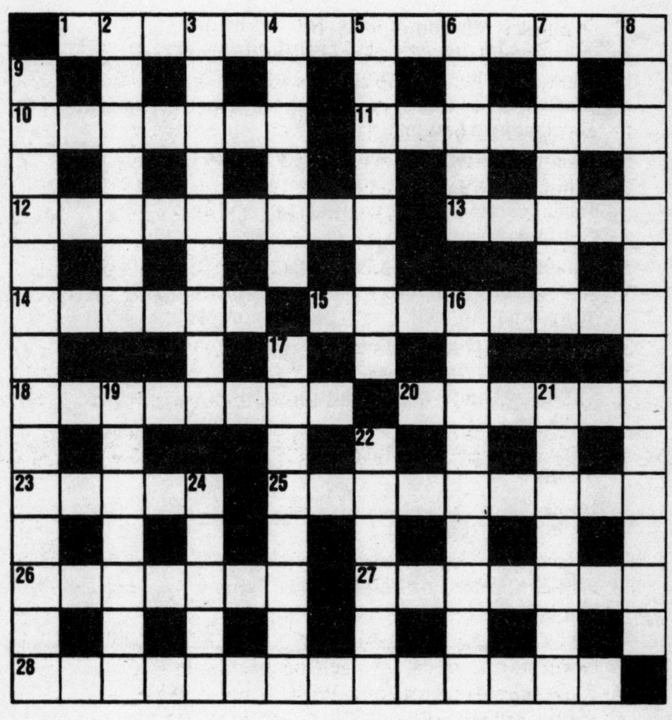

56

Across

1 No longer wanting frozen food at functions (7)
5 So a ring changes a girl's status in Rome (7)
9 Most woe-begotten couple (7)
10 Makes mistakes over a couple of points, so they are brought into action? (7)
11 Tenacious application for injury benefit (8, 7)
12 Steer a course as the crow flies (6)
14 Order canned fish – essential starters (8)
17 Settling on a plane trip? (6, 2)
18 Put on a vessel taking back a native to Australia (6)
21 Dickensian character we know and like (3, 6, 6)
24 Fly from hill-dweller with beastly companion (3-4)
25 Public entertainment almost wholly unethical (3-4)
26 Club magazine (7)
27 Cover girl had a meal in hospital (7)

Down

1 So bound to emigrate? (7)
2 Dry loofah irritated rash (9)
3 Blocks of wood worn out (5)
4 A record holder (6)
5 Chemicals spilled in water here, when ship split apart in stormy deep (5, 3)
6 Ram small Greek article on top of the stores (9)
7 Patent covering model (5)
8 Takes things in with a seaman's eyes (7)
13 A hundred on joining up displayed perplexity (9)
15 Untax beer? That could make us jolly lively! (9)
16 A mutual perplexity about first night of the season (8)
17 Or a part, maybe, in proportion (3, 4)
19 Confirm that object rose with difficulty (7)
20 Deceives more than one bank (6)
22 Painter fixed up estimates (5)
23 Sail along with compass (5)

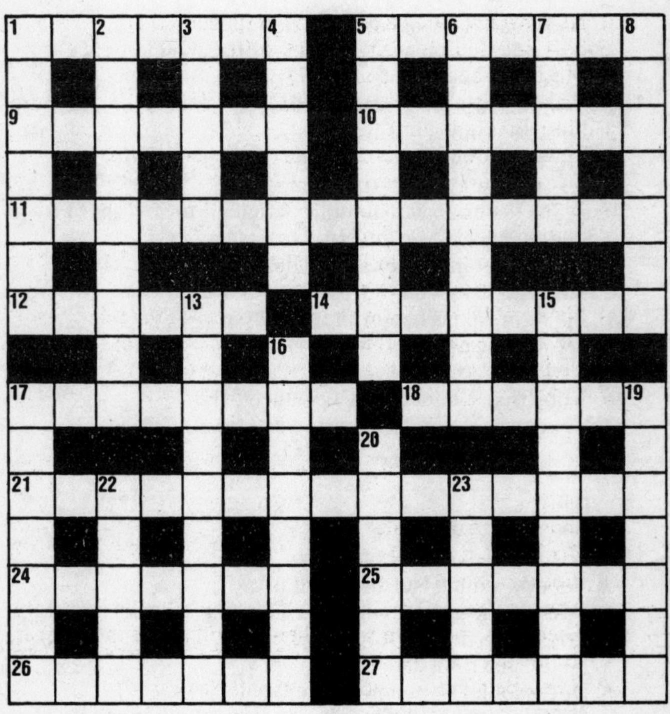

57

Across

1 Trade mark I dropped, flourished (10)
8 Brief account, then thanks, in the official minutes (4)
10 To become acceptable, discover a rosette, maybe (4, 6)
11 Uninteresting piece of scenery (4)
13 Obvious embarrassment when demand for silence interrupts song (7)
15 Girl is getting award – one pound (6)
16 Rogue teams up with upright character, to get fish (6)
17 Pledge given by the funeral contractors (4, 11)
18 Laid down pipe either side of the street (6)
20 Views making sense, Conservative held (6)
21 She was responsible for the power cut (7)
22 Before long one gets ahead (4)
25 Britannia succeeded where he failed (4, 6)
26 Scoop that sounds as if it's planned (4)
27 Newcomer's offer to infantrymen (10)

Down

2 Fire put out? It's out of control! (4)
3 Nobody joining Northern unit (4)
4 To close the gap initially I need fencing – ideally larch logs (6)
5 Be dressed for a date (4, 9, 2)
6 Ducks found by us among the rabbits (6)
7 Game seen to go different ways on higher ground (10)
9 Republicans ring doctor after Ian passes out (10)
12 Agree to write (10)
13 Half-drunk, one of the nine sisters has retired (7)
14 So trivial a wound is no handicap (7)
15 No standing on ceremony – tell a colleague (10)
19 Stop – there's a diversion to side street (6)
20 Salvation Army gave soup to the unconverted (6)
23 Wearing this of course you don't catch it (4)
24 Last letter returned with love means nothing (4)

57

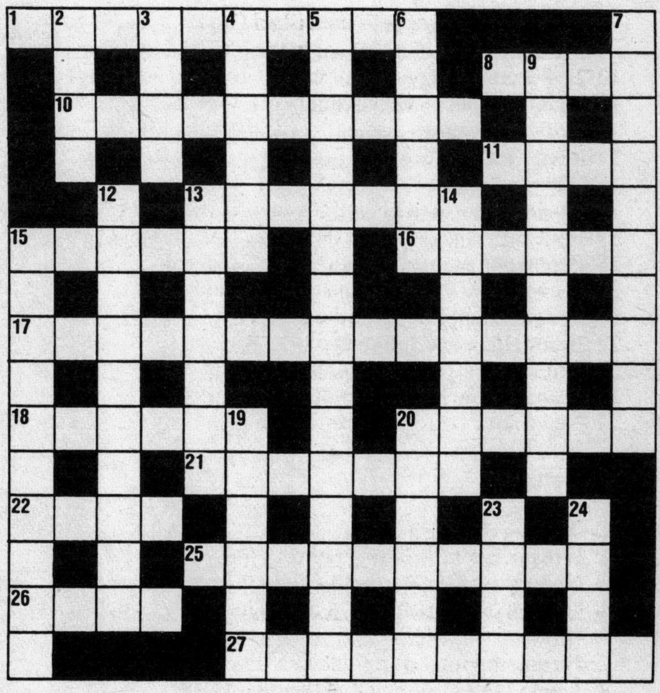

58

Across

1 Turning religious, at cross purposes perhaps (8)
5 Article on rights of foreigners (6)
9 Humans agree intellectually (8)
10 To communicate with a disc jockey, ring in (6)
12 Duck the Parisian consumed required salt (6)
13 Bottle opener always takes a long time, with drink required (8)
15 Broadcasting getting across to the embassy (12)
18 He would not light it up, during divine service (6-6)
23 Group holding money in a handkerchief (8)
24 Saint's home since goddess has retreated (6)
26 The purpose of binoculars (6)
27 26 across for updating? (8)
28 Way noxious weed can be cooked (6)
29 Border dispute dividing the land (8)

Down

1 One dog chasing another's woolly ball (6)
2 In the event editor came out with it (6)
3 To drag two-wheeled vehicle uphill? (7)
4 The bell tolling, it's said, for her (4)
6 Fifty snakes – what a game they have together (7)
7 The number one craze? (8)
8 Burning to warble a note in another key (8)
11 Where men get lost in the gloom? (7)
14 Fly the sovereign out about this time (7)
16 Plant promissary notes on the blackleg (8)
17 Set the river alight? It's an Arab habit (8)
19 Call for surrender of mace had to be modified (7)
20 Following points heading a legal petition (7)
21 Rank Princess held to be less of a mix-up (6)
22 Sort things out and achieve immediate success (6)
25 Measure a boundary (4)

58

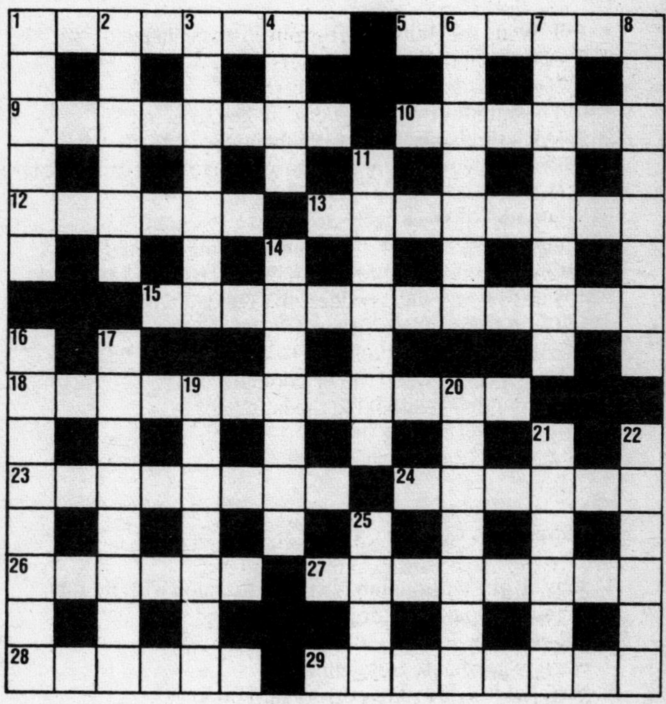

59

Across

1 But will he be a reliable one if this is what the player gives to his part? (10)
6 Mark backs the right bills (4)
9 Liqueur that turns gold (5)
10 Parking inside group long to find access to vessel (9)
12 Pocket animals sneakily? That's just what they might do (13)
14 Blind, like Shylock? (8)
15 A monster that's very strange in one way and another (6)
17 Enough at one time to achieve fame in the navy (6)
19 Flies apt to swarm to such scruffy public buildings? (4-4)
21 Tore spectator to pieces so lands in custody (13)
24 Team that won't be competing for the Wightman cup, by the sound of it (3, 6)
25 Cross that is holding sailor back (5)
26 Stop topless freedom from restraint (4)
27 To pull out could be shattering (10)

Down

1 A girl going without money but forearmed with this (4)
2 No need apparently for more towelling (3, 4)
3 Takes a turn for the better (8, 5)
4 Hard to get a note from him! (8)
5 Material for study I'm pursuing (5)
7 Men with guns in African country point at game (7)
8 In Sark she's turning to debauchery (10)
11 Once the cheapest form of transport? (5-8)
13 Very lights in key position – all spots visible (5, 5)
16 She takes religious instruction in a group at midday (8)
18 Abundance of food coming from the North (7)
20 Just a second – this is urgent (7)
22 In being diplomatic, I'll be silent (5)
23 Churchman – one in retreat (4)

60

Across

1 A procession – one that is held back in historic city (7)
5 As whips are reapplied, it's with intent to sting (7)
9 Express going north and further, carrying bags back (3-4)
10 A practical person is alert at sea (7)
11 Brief personal details provided by letters from a vessel (9, 6)
12 Fish from the deep freeze? (6)
14 Wrecked on an island inhabited by birds (8)
17 Passed on, but still has a share in the action (8)
18 Stop marine slaughter (6)
21 Borough with palm path – intriguing setting for snappy book (10, 5)
24 Frank confusing increase with a loss (7)
25 Hold damaged tin can – empty (7)
26 Top worker holding Doctor of Divinity to be small fish (7)
27 The remainder live around the bend (7)

Down

1 Criticize expert with a cure (7)
2 Adequate supplies of underwear, proverbially (4, 1, 4)
3 Overcast actor? (5)
4 Suggest I, the person indicated, should get in place (6)
5 Somewhat hot – door's open in the mess (8)
6 Marine hazard, so listen at bridgehead in position (5, 4)
7 Tom-noddy and I do it, up the creek (5)
8 Deliver an upper-cut here in the Home Counties? (7)
13 Material is one with stripes and everyone's in it (9)
15 Distinguished directors? That's right (9)
16 Doubly attentive to the applause? (4-4)
17 The first payment I posted off, probably (7)
19 The man who's proposed (7)
20 Bar for typists (6)
22 Confessed to having been in possession (5)
23 She takes an inordinately long time grasping the point (5)

Solutions

No. 1

Across: 1, Handbook; 5, Gets up; 9, Pugilist; 10, Matron; 12, Noting; 13, Slapdash; 15, Delicatessen; 18, Disconsolate; 23, Moulders; 24, Strata; 26, Tiered; 27, Occasion; 28, Rating; 29, Junk-shop.

Down: 1, Hoping; 2, Negate; 3, Balance; 4, Ouse; 6, Example; 7, Sargasso; 8, Penchant; 11, Pliably; 14, Fissure; 16, Odometer; 17, Esculent; 19, Old bean; 20, Titlark; 21, Vanish; 22, Cat-nap; 25, Ecru.

No. 2

Across: 4, Steerage; 8, Deluge; 9, Tenement; 10, Duellist; 11, Tissot; 12, Relegate; 13, Original; 16, Portrait; 19, Hatchway; 21, Astrid; 23, Straddle; 24, Tranship; 25, Agreed; 26, Tea-chest.

Down: 1, Reputed; 2, Guillemot; 3, Retina; 4, Settle on the spot; 5, Einstein; 6, Remus; 7, Gondola; 14, In the dark; 15, Sand-shoe; 17, Observe; 18, Dallies; 20, Thread; 22, Runic.

No. 3

Across: 1, Just as well; 6, Know; 9, Yodel; 10, Linklater; 12, Light-fingered; 14, Portends; 15, Millet; 17, Cloche; 19, Quagmire; 21, Anti-apartheid; 24, Landscape; 25, Imago; 26, So-so; 27, Raised Cain.

Down: 1, Jays; 2, Saddler; 3, At loggerheads; 4, Well-to-do; 5, Lungi; 7, Natural; 8, Ward duties; 11, Lagging behind; 13, Spectacles; 16, Buttress; 18, Outings; 20, Indiana; 22, Agama; 23, Loon.

No. 4

Across: 1, Tasting; 5, Cantrip; 9, Aconite; 10, Annular; 11, Fleeting glances; 12, Cretan; 14, Integral; 17, Offshoot; 18, Placed; 21, Payment received; 24, Staging; 25, Observe; 26, Donegal; 27, Saladin.

Down: 1, Traffic; 2, Stone-deaf; 3, Idiot; 4, Greens; 5, Changing; 6, Nonpareil; 7, Relic; 8, Perusal; 13, Achieving; 15, Recovered; 16, Portugal; 17, Opposed; 19, Dudgeon; 20, Herons; 22, Yearn; 23, Easel.

No. 5

Across: 1, Arthurian legend; 9, Hair-net; 10, Imputes; 11, Dado; 12, Autostrada; 13, Goliath; 15, Eritrea; 17, Depress; 19, Theatre; 20, Immaterial; 22, Diva; 25, Enthuse; 26, Nineveh; 27, Stocks and shares.

Down: 1, Aphid; 2, Third slip; 3, Ulna; 4, In touch; 5, Noisome; 6, Empathise; 7, Extra; 8, Disparate; 13, Godliness; 14, Awe-struck; 16, Retriever; 18, Seriema; 19, Trained; 21, Motto; 23, Ashes; 24, Inch.

No. 6

Across: 1, Backlash; 5, Relief; 9, Archives; 10, Enzyme; 12, Drogue; 13, Furbelow; 15, Regardlessly; 18, Turn down a bed; 23, Leadenly; 24, Adagio; 26, In-tray; 27, Overcome; 28, Neaten; 29, All's well.

Down: 1, Brands; 2, Cocoon; 3, Leisure; 4, Suez; 6, Ennoble; 7, Icy blast; 8, Freeways; 11, Sundial; 14, Cat-walk; 16, Stallion; 17, Cream tea; 19, Due care; 20, Endures; 21, Ignore; 22, Nowell; 25, Oval.

No. 7

Across: 1, Medicate; 5, Couple; 9, Platinum; 10, Clinic; 12, Shelf; 13, Bookstall; 14, Philanthrope; 18, Elliptically; 21, Poignancy; 23, Arena; 24, Amulet; 25, Sinister; 26, Eleven; 27, Deckhand.

Down: 1, Mopish; 2, Diadem; 3, Chiefship; 4, Tourbillions; 6, Ogles; 7, Pentagon; 8, Excelled; 11, Boundary line; 15, Half a tick; 16, Keepsake; 17, Altitude; 19, Bertha; 20, Hatred; 22, Niece.

No. 8

Across: 1, Transportation; 10, Enteron; 11, Adamant; 12, Pinchbars; 13, Yahoo; 14, Cravat; 15, Habanera; 18, Appetite; 20, Acacia; 23, Inapt; 25, Latescent; 26, Inexact; 27, Airline; 28, Youth-hosteller.

Down: 2, Rotunda; 3, North-east; 4, Punjab; 5, Rear seat; 6, Ataxy; 7, Ivanhoe; 8, National anthem; 9, Respectability; 16, Ancestral; 17, Stiletto; 19, Plateau; 21, Chemise; 22, At last; 24, Trash.

No. 9

Across: 1, Remnant; 5, Sublime; 9, Fistula; 10, Antwerp; 11, Acute depression; 12, Nailed; 14, Apple pie; 17, Cheating; 18, Tsetse; 21, Under the weather; 24, Alabama; 25, Pibroch; 26, Eleanor; 27, Doe-skin.

Down: 1, Refrain; 2, Masculine; 3, Acute; 4, Tracer; 5, Sea-trips; 6, Bath salts; 7, Iceni; 8, Expense; 13, Entertain; 15, Pitch-fork; 16, In the air; 17, Courage; 19, Earthen; 20, Swiped; 22, Drake; 23, Amble.

No. 10

Across: 4, Careless; 8, Hither; 9, Obdurate; 10, Shamrock; 11, Amazon; 12, Declared; 13, Oscitant; 16, Barnacle; 19, Splinter; 21, Patent; 23, Omission; 24, Waterloo; 25, Eleven; 26, Straddle.

Down: 1, Lighter; 2, Chameleon; 3, Armour; 4, Cooked one's goose; 5, Radiance; 6, Larva; 7, Set down; 14, Tarnished; 15, Scuttled; 17, Adamant; 18, Denoted; 20, Loiter; 22, Enema.

No. 11

Across: 1, Saturnalia; 8, Gaga; 10, Alarmingly; 11, Fail; 13, Mélange; 15, Anchor; 16, Enamel; 17, Robin Goodfellow; 18, Redeem; 20, Tracer; 21, Dithers; 22, Suva; 25, Will of iron; 26, Ezra; 27, New Zealand.

Down: 2, Atap; 3, Upas; 4, Number; 5, Long arm of the law; 6, Allege; 7, Wallflower; 9, Alarm-clock; 12, Scuba diver; 13, Mounted; 14, Endears; 15, Air-brushed; 19, Minion; 20, Trifle; 23, Oral; 24, Anon.

No. 12

Across: 1, Castanet; 5, Catsup; 9, Remedied; 10, Errant; 12, Theory; 13, Dispense; 15, Enthusiastic; 18, Brassfounder; 23, Diatribe; 24, Assume; 26, Editor; 27, Internal; 28, Tisane; 29, Maintain.

Down: 1, Curate; 2, Summer; 3, Andiron; 4, Ewer; 6, Agrippa; 7, Stagnate; 8, Patience; 11, Dissent; 14, Theorbo; 16, Obedient; 17, Canaries; 19, Sirloin; 20, Eastern; 21, Duenna; 22, Merlin; 25, Inca.

No. 13

Across: 1, Peregrine Pickle; 9, Impeach; 10, Laid out; 11, Ebro; 12, Propaganda; 13, Project; 15, Elastic; 17, Cry wolf; 19, Resoled; 20, Discourage; 22, Ogle; 25, Ironing; 26, Orchard; 27, Lithe as a panther.

Down: 1, Prime; 2, Repertory; 3, Gnat; 4, Inherit; 5, Ellipse; 6, Isinglass; 7, Known; 8, Entranced; 13, Pack-drill; 14, Economise; 16, Telegraph; 18, Forages; 19, Regroup; 21, Shoot; 23, Eider; 24, Scan.

No. 14

Across: 1, Coordinates; 10, Optic; 11, Water-polo; 12, Dire peril; 13, Hiems; 14, Nodose; 16, Spitfire; 18, First aid; 20, Tannin; 23, Owner; 24, President; 26, Teenagers; 27, Torso; 28, Roast turkey.

Down: 2, Ottar; 3, Recipes; 4, Inward; 5, Antelope; 6, Earshot; 7, Cold and frosty; 8, Bohemian; 9, Consternation; 15, Deranged; 17, Tie-press; 19, Tornado; 21, Aviator; 22, Tea-set; 25, Eerie.

No. 15

Across: 1, Orpheus; 5, Evictor; 9, Unnerve; 10, Cypress; 11, Anthropological; 12, Enlist; 14, Detector; 17, Examiner; 18, Ascent; 21, Cross the Rubicon; 24, Arizona; 25, Timpani; 26, Engulfs; 27, Abetter.

Down: 1, Oculate; 2, Panatella; 3, Error; 4, Sherpa; 5, Excelled; 6, Impugners; 7, Theic; 8, Rustler; 13, Swiss roll; 15, Trenchant; 16, Red-heads; 17, Enclave; 19, Tangier; 20, Protea; 22, Owing; 23, Bombe.

No. 16

Across: 1, Castle in the air; 10, Exigent; 11, Break up; 12, Speedwell; 13, Somme; 14, With it; 15, Purchase; 18, Yodeller; 20, Russet; 23, Ictus; 25, Greatcoat; 26, Harrier; 27, Locarno; 28, The Lord's Prayer.

Down: 2, Aliment; 3, Treadmill; 4, Either; 5, Nebulous; 6, Heels; 7, Ack-emma; 8, Representation; 9, Gets away with it; 16, Crustacea; 17, Beggared; 19, Deterge; 21, Scourge; 22, Dewlap; 24, Sligo.

No. 17

Across: 1, Scrabble; 5, Spider; 9, Valencia; 10, Set off; 12, Re-echo; 13, Balinese; 15, Astonishment; 18, Recriminated; 23, Slipshod; 24, Isabel; 26, Alegar; 27, Asbestos; 28, Estate; 29, Magnesia.

Down: 1, Severe; 2, Roller; 3, Bunches; 4, Laid; 6, Pie-dish; 7, Diogenes; 8, Reflects; 11, Habitat; 14, Monitor; 16, Dressage; 17, Accident; 19, Instant; 20, Eastern; 21, Abatis; 22, Alaska; 25, Ossa.

No. 18

Across: 1, Comparison; 8, Opal; 10, Australian; 11, Wait; 13, Slander; 15, Laxity; 16, Repeal; 17, Dollar diplomacy; 18, Spirit; 20, Reader; 21, Crooner; 22, Oxen; 25, Hard labour; 26, Esse; 27, Tuning-fork.

Down: 2, Olaf; 3, Pass; 4, Rarely; 5, Silence is golden; 6, Neater; 7, Plate-layer; 9, Place-cards; 12, Exploiters; 13, Stearic; 14, Recover; 15, Lodestones; 19, Truant; 20, Regain; 23, Woof; 24, Brer.

No. 19

Across: 1, Material; 5, Abuses; 9, Doubting; 10, Player; 12, Scales; 13, Aspirate; 15, Sticky wicket; 18, Prosecutions; 23, Remotely; 24, Strafe; 26, Inroad; 27, Manatees; 28, Events; 29, Dovetail.

Down: 1, Modest; 2, Toucan; 3, Retreat; 4, Anna; 6, Bellini; 7, Skylarks; 8, Serpents; 11, Assyria; 14, Scruple; 16, Sportive; 17, Commerce; 19, Extract; 20, Nitrate; 21, Zareba; 22, Weasel; 25, Iago.

No. 20

Across: 1, Pathologist; 10, Alien; 11, Procreate; 12, Gravesend; 13, Optic; 14, Nazism; 16, Lava-lava; 18, Hoof-beat; 20, Missal; 23, Ha-has; 24, Basilicon; 26, Astraddle; 27, Rolls; 28, Incarnadine.

Down: 2, Anima; 3, Hunters; 4, Lapped; 5, Good deal; 6, Sarcoma; 7, Bang on the head; 8, Martians; 9, Teachableness; 15, Zoophyte; 17, Cambodia; 19, Bestain; 21, Ill-bred; 22, Astern; 25, Colin.

No. 21

Across: 1, Foreman; 5, Cabinet; 9, Lost dog; 10, Latrine; 11, Indomitableness; 12, Gentry; 14, Steelman; 17, Blessing; 18, Idling; 21, Photograph album; 24, Agonist; 25, Chicago; 26, Emerged; 27, Epicene.

Down: 1, Falling; 2, Residence; 3, Madam; 4, Negate; 5, Celibate; 6, Bitter end; 7, Noise; 8, Treason; 13, Restoring; 15, Mainbrace; 16, Uncrated; 17, Biplane; 19, Gamboge; 20, Apache; 22, Ozone; 23, Alibi.

No. 22

Across: 1, Colorado; 5, Profit; 9, Birettas; 10, Stir up; 12, Exotic; 13, Grenades; 15, Yellow-hammer; 18, Schoolmaster; 23, Ant-lions; 24, Stayed; 26, Llamas; 27, Holidays; 28, Putrid; 29, Diastema.

Down: 1, Cobweb; 2, Lardon; 3, Ratline; 4, Draw; 6, Rotunda; 7, Firedamp; 8, Tapestry; 11, Prowess; 14, Alimony; 16, Escallop; 17, White ant; 19, Origami; 20, Entries; 21, Aye-aye; 22, Odessa; 25, Gobi.

No. 23

Across: 1, Parallelograms; 10, Hearten; 11, Blossom; 12, Main force; 13, Eagre; 14, Insect; 15, Stiffish; 18, Leg-break; 20, Global; 23, Adult; 25, Dart-board; 26, Hyalite; 27, Granary; 28, Reintroduction.

Down: 2, Ananias; 3, Artificer; 4, Lanark; 5, Libretto; 6, Glove; 7, Assagai; 8, Summer holidays; 9, Chamois leather; 16, Full blast; 17, San Diego; 19, Gourami; 21, Bravado; 22, Gru-gru; 24, Twist.

No. 24

Across: 4, Starling; 8, Gillie; 9, Proverbs; 10, Derelict; 11, Exhale; 12, Prunella; 13, Golconda; 16, Venetian; 19, Alopecia; 21, Dalasi; 23, Inaction; 24, Dalmatia; 25, Livery; 26, Ventures.

Down: 1, Firearm; 2, Alternate; 3, Refill; 4, Septuagenarians; 5, Above all; 6, Leech; 7, Nobbled; 14, Objective; 15, Sinister; 17, Emanate; 18, Bigotry; 20, Orally; 22, Admit.

No. 25

Across: 1, Playwright; 6, Atap; 9, Styli; 10, Elucidate; 12, Schoolmasters; 14, Numerate; 15, Platan; 17, Editor; 19, Drabbler; 21, Redevelopment; 24, Extortion; 25, Elite; 26, Toss; 27, Persistent.

Down: 1, Past; 2, Alyssum; 3, Whithersoever; 4, Ice-boats; 5, Haulm; 7, Tea-tent; 8, Pleasantry; 11, Insolubleness; 13, Endearment; 16, Gropings; 18, Indites; 20, Lattice; 22, Loire; 23, Vent.

No. 26

Across: 1, Laconic; 5, Embargo; 9, Utopian; 10, Profuse; 11, Descending order; 12, Stylet; 14, Benjamin; 17, Redstart; 18, Oberon; 21, Never a cross word; 24, Holdall; 25, Tearful; 26, Stained; 27, Starter.

Down: 1, Lourdes; 2, Cross-eyed; 3, Naïve; 4, Canada; 5, Expander; 6, Book of Job; 7, Round; 8, Overrun; 13, Entertain; 15, Marrowfat; 16, Truckled; 17, Ranches; 19, Nodular; 20, Coitus; 22, Villa; 23, Scala.

No. 27

Across: 1, Good turn; 5, Heroic; 9, Decrease; 10, Weldon; 12, Whimsy; 13, Filigree; 15, Interrogates; 18, Mixed doubles; 23, Silencer; 24, Hinder; 26, Inches; 27, Beatrice; 28, Gitano; 29, Wardress.

Down: 1, Godown; 2, Orchid; 3, Treason; 4, Rest; 6, Evening; 7, Obdurate; 8, Converse; 11, Microbe; 14, Reposed; 16, Smashing; 17, Explicit; 19, Dungeon; 20, Existed; 21, Advice; 22, Creels; 25, Mesa.

No. 28

Across: 1, Hippodrome; 8, Apse; 10, Informally; 11, Bran; 13, Hengist; 15, Pieman; 16, Tremor; 17, Demonstratively; 18, Insist; 20, Aerial; 21, Seaside; 22, Grit; 25, Invalidate; 26, Aces; 27, Stevedores.

Down: 2, Ibid; 3, Puff; 4, Darken; 5, Orange Free State; 6, Enlist; 7, Pennyroyal; 9, Paramnesia; 12, Permissive; 13, Harness; 14, Trainee; 15, Pudding-bag; 19, Tennis; 20, Advise; 23, Dado; 24, Mere.

No. 29

Across: 1, Vice-presidents; 10, Richard; 11, Entitle; 12, Sassolite; 13, Sibyl; 14, Inroad; 15, Rock-hewn; 18, Gardenia; 20, Hyssop; 23, Humus; 25, Amazonian; 26, Braille; 27, Abridge; 28, Retain the Ashes.

Down: 2, Incisor; 3, Elaborate; 4, Reduit; 5, Skeleton; 6, Dates; 7, Notable; 8, Shetland ponies; 9, Crossing the bar; 16, Keyboards; 17, Filament; 19, Rampant; 21, Swindle; 22, Palate; 24, Solti.

No. 30

Across: 4, All at sea; 8, Pelota; 9, Pavement; 10, Cocktail; 11, Redact; 12, Demoniac; 13, Heirless; 16, Bachelor; 19, Long-stop; 21, Urchin; 23, Tapeworm; 24, Overcast; 25, Lashes; 26, Oddments.

Down: 1, Recover; 2, Cockroach; 3, Salami; 4, Apple charlottes; 5, Live rail; 6, Timid; 7, Eunuchs; 14, Leastwise; 15, Plantain; 17, Arrived; 18, Courser; 20, Napalm; 22, Harem.

No. 31

Across: 1, Obviate; 5, Rackets; 9, Nocuous; 10, Lacquer; 11, Bolt from the blue; 12, Staffa; 14, Pothooks; 17, Died away; 18, Stocks; 21, Soft-heartedness; 24, Illyria; 25, Philtre; 26, Emended; 27, Emerald.

Down: 1, Omnibus; 2, Vacillate; 3, Aloof; 4, Euston; 5, Relation; 6, Cocked hat; 7, Equal; 8, Servers; 13, Feathered; 15, Orchestra; 16, Saraband; 17, Despite; 19, Suspend; 20, Staple; 22, False; 23, Drive.

No. 32

Across: 1, Tell-tale; 5, Cha-cha; 9, Alastair; 10, Slates; 12, Cleans; 13, Rambling; 15, Acquaintance; 18, Constituents; 23, Reorient; 24, Estate; 26, Banner; 27, Gulliver; 28, Egesta; 29, Chess-set.

Down: 1, Thatch; 2, Leaven; 3, Titanic; 4, Lair; 6, Halibut; 7, Catriona; 8, Assignee; 11, Matinee; 14, Mustang; 16, Scarabee; 17, Announce; 19, Trident; 20, Tussles; 21, Calves; 22, Regret; 25, Ruth.

No. 33

Across: 1, Sidecars; 5, Masses; 9, Doldrums; 10, Appear; 12, Night; 13, Normalise; 14, Abbreviation; 18, Forked tongue; 21, Leaves off; 23, Excel; 24, Exiled; 25, Freehold; 26, Tennis; 27, Mentally.

Down: 1, Siding; 2, Deluge; 3, Card-table; 4, Remuneration; 6, Alpha; 7, Specific; 8, Sergeant; 11, Driving force; 15, Amusement; 16, Affluent; 17, Creation; 19, School; 20, Gladly; 22, Elemi.

No. 34

Across: 1, Disadvantageous; 9, Ampulla; 10, Ernesto; 11, Hook; 12, Vice-consul; 13, Detente; 15, Nodding; 17, Springs; 19, Parapet; 20, Conveyance; 22, Mere; 25, Amnesia; 26, Adamant; 27, Eternal devotion.

Down: 1, Death; 2, Supporter; 3, Dolt; 4, Avarice; 5, Therein; 6, Gunpowder; 7, Ousts; 8, Spotlight; 13, Desecrate; 14, Nonperson; 16, Impresari; 18, Sea-wall; 19, Package; 21, Nonce; 23, Eaten; 24, Faro.

No. 35

Across: 1, Knapper; 5, Fish-net; 9, Elation; 10, Moidore; 11, Lightning strike; 12, Nassau; 14, Et cetera; 17, Charisma; 18, Tsetse; 21, Dog with two tails; 24, Italics; 25, Vintage; 26, Eponyms; 27, Lantern.

Down: 1, Kremlin; 2, Analgesia; 3, Point; 4, Runcie; 5, Fumigate; 6, Shiftless; 7, Naomi; 8, Theresa; 13, Asininity; 15, Extricate; 16, Emphasis; 17, Codeine; 19, Eastern; 20, Swivel; 22, Guano; 23, Tenon.

No. 36

Across: 1, Sound-track; 6, Scar; 9, Glass; 10, Dayspring; 12, Knows full well; 14, Bedecked; 15, Aslant; 17, Odours; 19, Colophon; 21, Putting-greens; 24, Immigrant; 25, Hoist; 26, Nana; 27, Snapdragon.

Down: 1, Sage; 2, Unasked; 3, Disconcerting; 4, Radishes; 5, Coypu; 7, Chimera; 8, Regulating; 11, Pulls together; 13, Absorption; 16, Doorstop; 18, Ottoman; 20, Husking; 22, Grain; 23, Sten.

No. 37

Across: 1, Tactical; 5, Scorch; 9, Coiffure; 10, Tic-tac; 12, Liners; 13, Gangrene; 15, Concentrated; 18, Acceleration; 23, Churlish; 24, Clause; 26, Elixir; 27, Spanking; 28, Engage; 29, Schooner.

Down: 1, Tackle; 2, Cairns; 3, Inferno; 4, Airy; 6, Chigger; 7, Retreats; 8, Hacienda; 11, Magneto; 14, Actress; 16, Marchese; 17, Scouring; 19, Lolling; 20, Orlando; 21, Fusion; 22, Verger; 25, Epic.

No. 38

Across: 1, Mustard plaster; 10, Acheron; 11, Oarsman; 12, Ernestine; 13, Duomo; 14, Irenic; 15, Itemised; 18, Turmeric; 20, Tsampa; 23, Exact; 25, Wonderful; 26, Orifice; 27, Drop off; 28, Demoralisation.

Down: 2, Unhinge; 3, Turnstile; 4, Rancid; 5, Property; 6, Aired; 7, Tomboys; 8, Ran for dear life; 9, Babes in the wood; 16, Misses out; 17, Pin-wheel; 19, Realism; 21, Mafioso; 22, Anodes; 24, Trier.

No. 39

Across: 1, Test-tube; 5, Balsam; 9, Abstract; 10, Damask; 12, Lemma; 13, Leaves off; 14, Panel-beaters; 18, Flying saucer; 21, Eroticism; 23, Dream; 24, Ice-cap; 25, Austrian; 26, Gander; 27, Thistles.

Down: 1, Trails; 2, Sesame; 3, Turn again; 4, Becalmed ship; 6, Abase; 7, Shadowed; 8, Make fast; 11, Harbour mouth; 15, Anecdotes; 16, Offering; 17, Tyrolean; 19, Genial; 20, Amends; 22, Image.

No. 40

Across: 1, Verglas; 5, Paragon; 9, Nobbily; 10, Ousting; 11, Sound investment; 12, Nodose; 14, Idolises; 17, Redrafts; 18, Adonis; 21, First impression; 24, Lucerne; 25, Express; 26, Spondee; 27, Dilates.

Down: 1, Venison; 2, Rebounded; 3, Laird; 4, Saying; 5, Proceeds; 6, Resettled; 7, Guide; 8, Negates; 13, Shattered; 15, Sentiment; 16, Stampede; 17, Raffles; 19, Sinuses; 20, Friend; 22, Recto; 23, Sepal.

No. 41

Across: 1, Gesticulate; 10, Rouse; 11, Upper hand; 12, Impressed; 13, Uredo; 14, Isobar; 16, Green tea; 18, Gift book; 20, Nuclei; 23, Outer; 24, Jacaranda; 26, Registrar; 27, Vocal; 28, Shareholder.

Down: 2, Equip; 3, Theresa; 4, Course; 5, Lapidary; 6, Torture; 7, Draining-board; 8, Parental; 9, Idiomatically; 15, Off-stage; 17, Conjuror; 19, Bortsch; 21, Unravel; 22, Scorch; 25, Niche.

No. 42

Across: 1, Fragment; 5, Bantam; 9, Listless; 10, Moaned; 12, Number; 13, Liniment; 15, Astonishment; 18, Entertaining; 23, Barbaric; 24, Twinge; 26, Arctic; 27, Angelica; 28, Ensign; 29, Interest.

Down: 1, Filing; 2, Assume; 3, Millers; 4, Nose; 6, Abolish; 7, Tendered; 8, Meditate; 11, Pinions; 14, Botanic; 16, Membrane; 17, Attracts; 19, Reading; 20, Nowhere; 21, Incite; 22, Repast; 25, Anon.

No. 43

Across: 1; Determined; 8, Leda; 10, Clementine; 11, Scut; 13, Merited; 15, Dollar; 16, Yellow; 17, Loch Ness Monster; 18, Vaults; 20, Melons; 21, Open air; 22, Rota; 25, Petitioner; 26, Nest; 27, Egg custard.

Down: 2, Etch; 3, Even; 4, Meeker; 5, Notwithstanding; 6, Donkey; 7, Earthworms; 9, Escalation; 12, Fluctuates; 13, Magneto; 14, Dernier; 15, Delivering; 19, Sphere; 20, Milieu; 23, Unit; 24, Brer.

No. 44

Across: 1, Deplete; 5, Bugloss; 9, Fancier; 10, Cursive; 11, Canterbury bells; 12, Sturdy; 14, Fall open; 17, Heathrow; 18, Sierra; 21, Yield to the touch; 24, Emanate; 25, Rainier; 26, Scenery; 27, Ebriety.

Down: 1, Defects; 2, Peninsula; 3, Exile; 4, Enrobe; 5, Bactrian; 6, Garibaldi; 7, Oriel; 8, Stepson; 13, Dehydrate; 15, Porcupine; 16, Jocosely; 17, Hoydens; 19, Ash-tray; 20, Charge; 22, Evade; 23, Trier.

No. 45

Across: 1, Steamships; 6, Comb; 9, Roger; 10, Shipboard; 12, Spit and polish; 14, Benjamin; 15, Redeem; 17, Retape; 19, Fishcake; 21, Gladstone bags; 24, New Jersey; 25, Trump; 26, Lays; 27, Candidates.

Down: 1, Surf; 2, Egg us on; 3, Marzipan paste; 4, Hispanic; 5, Pried; 7, Opaline; 8, Bedchamber; 11, Broken-hearted; 13, Aboriginal; 16, Wide-eyed; 18, Tramway; 20, Assault; 22, Ossia; 23, Opts.

No. 46

Across: 1, Manifold; 5, Normal; 9, Rock-rose; 10, Agouti; 12, Nougat; 13, Cornetto; 15, Colour scheme; 18, Mistranslate; 23, Overturn; 24, Object; 26, Isobar; 27, Protract; 28, Endued; 29, Assailed.

Down: 1, Marina; 2, Noctua; 3, Farrago; 4, List; 6, Organic; 7, Mounties; 8, Laid open; 11, Courtly; 14, Joiners; 16, Immobile; 17, Asteroid; 19, Retrace; 20, Tabitha; 21, Retail; 22, Stated; 25, Iris.

No. 47

Across: 1, Gall and wormwood; 9, Grocery; 10, Solders; 11, Toad; 12, Winchester; 13, Intense; 15, Embassy; 17, Pyramid; 19, Fielder; 20, Our betters; 22, Visa; 25, Portico; 26, Opposer; 27, Unrighteousness.

Down: 1, Gigot; 2, Look after; 3, Apex; 4, Daytime; 5, Ossicle; 6, Malleable; 7, Overt; 8, Destroyer; 13, Impromptu; 14, Numbering; 16, Side issue; 18, Detroit; 19, Furioso; 21, Rarer; 23, Arras; 24, Opus.

No. 48

Across: 1, Familiar; 5, Cantab; 9, Ring back; 10, Tautog; 12, Arena; 13, Matriarch; 14, Billingsgate; 18, Apron strings; 21, Plainsong; 23, Evade; 24, Inured; 25, Nagasaki; 26, Tie-dye; 27, Streaker.

Down: 1, Format; 2, Monkey; 3, Librarian; 4, Accumulation; 6, Amati; 7, Tutorial; 8, Big wheel; 11, Standing fast; 15, Segregate; 16, War paint; 17, Creature; 19, Damask; 20, Metier; 22, Needy.

No. 49

Across: 1, Whiplash; 5, Amused; 9, Explicit; 10, Altair; 12, Cocoon; 13, Buddleia; 15, Steeplechase; 18, Incarcerates; 23, Taffrail; 24, Appeal; 26, Climbs; 27, Threaded; 28, Sights; 29, Two-steps.

Down: 1, Wrench; 2, Impact; 3, Laid out; 4, Slit; 6, Melodic; 7, Spaceman; 8, Dark Ages; 11, Pullman; 14, Heretic; 16, Tin-tacks; 17, Scoffing; 19, Rarebit; 20, Express; 21, Beadle; 22, Glides; 25, Chow.

No. 50

Across: 1, Dress-circle; 10, Nadia; 11, Recondite; 12, Overgrown; 13, Untie; 14, Violet; 16, Clarinet; 18, Duckling; 20, Gâteau; 23, Rioja; 24, Extortion; 26, Maelstrom; 27, Oasis; 28, Inadvertent.

Down: 2, Ridge; 3, Spangle; 4, Cordon; 5, Recently; 6, Languor; 7, Unsolved crime; 8, Distance; 9, Deceitfulness; 15, Once-over; 17, Interred; 19, Liaison; 21, Airport; 22, Stymie; 25, Ibsen.

No. 51

Across: 1, Fireside; 5, Tragic; 9, Capering; 10, Smears; 12, Odium; 13, Emanation; 14, Constituents; 18, Winding sheet; 21, Enchilada; 23, Reach; 24, Ice Age; 25, Etchings; 26, Gasket; 27, Dyed blue.

Down: 1, Factor; 2, Repair; 3, Stromboli; 4, Danger signal; 6, Rumba; 7, Gradient; 8, Cosiness; 11, Danish pastry; 15, Unearthed; 16, Sweeping; 17, Knickers; 19, Carnal; 20, Chaste; 22, Ingle.

No. 52

Across: 1, Inferno; 5, Warfare; 9, Pursuit; 10, Raddled; 11, Catch as catch can; 12, Sylvan; 14, Incisors; 17, Impetigo; 18, Unseat; 21, Castles in the air; 24, Bar-bell; 25, Erosion; 26, Samoyed; 27, Tear-gas.

Down: 1, Impacts; 2, First slip; 3, Rough; 4, Obtuse; 5, War paint; 6, Redaction; 7, Aulic; 8, Endings; 13, Artillery; 15, Operating; 16, Egg salad; 17, Incubus; 19, Tyrants; 20, Indent; 22, Sarum; 23, Hooka.

No. 53

Across: 1, Misspent; 5, Stumer; 9, Brigands; 10, Betrim; 12, Legate; 13, Bassinet; 15, Predominates; 18, Addle-brained; 23, Theorise; 24, Maroon; 26, Elixir; 27, Haymaker; 28, Sledge; 29, Housetop.

Down: 1, Mobile; 2, Stingy; 3, Psalter; 4, Node; 6, Treason; 7, Marinate; 8, Remotest; 11, Barmaid; 14, Address; 16, Fastness; 17, Adhesive; 19, Earring; 20, Erasmus; 21, Pocket; 22, Unwrap; 25, Halo.

No. 54

Across: 1, Punishment; 6, Grim; 9, Punch; 10, Rendering; 12, Protectorates; 14, Windmill; 15, Sharer; 17, Nudism; 19, Redolent; 21, Pattern-makers; 24, Innisfree; 25, Ennui; 26, Goes; 27, Fever trees.

Down: 1, Pupa; 2, Ninepin; 3, Schoolmasters; 4, Martello; 5, Nonet; 7, Roister; 8, Magistrate; 11, Earth movement; 13, Swan-upping; 16, Nepalese; 18, Detente; 20, Essence; 22, Nurse; 23, Vies.

No. 55

Across: 1, Marching orders; 10, Piccolo; 11, October; 12, Cormorant. 13, Siren; 14, Tie-pin; 15, Annigoni; 18, Answered; 20, Sprout; 23, Eliot; 25, Sea-breeze; 26, Largish; 27, Chapati; 28, Right about turn.

Down: 2, Accurse; 3, Crocodile; 4, Isobar; 5, Grouting; 6, Rates; 7, Embargo; 8, Spring in the air; 9, Space traveller; 16, Important; 17, Memsahib; 19, Skin rug; 21, Open air; 22, Manchu; 24, Twist.

No. 56

Across: 1, Offices; 5, Signora; 9, Twosome; 10, Erasers; 11, Adhesive plaster; 12, Direct; 14, Tidiness; 17, Paying up; 18, Assume; 21, Our Mutual Friend; 24, Ant-lion; 25, Fun-fair; 26, Arsenal; 27, Sheathe.

Down: 1, Outward; 2, Foolhardy; 3, Clogs; 4, Sleeve; 5, Sheep dip; 6, Granaries; 7, Overt; 8, Absorbs; 13, Confusion; 15, Exuberant; 16, Autumnal; 17, Pro rata; 19, Endorse; 20, Bluffs; 22, Rates; 23, Range.

No. 57

Across: 1, Brandished; 8, Acta; 10, Find favour; 11, Flat; 13, Blushes; 15, Isobel; 16, Scampi; 17, Firm undertaking; 18, Rested; 20, Scenes; 21, Delilah; 22, Anon; 25, King Canute; 26, Lade; 27, Tenderfoot.

Down: 2, Rife; 3, None; 4, Infill; 5, Have something on; 6, Douses; 7, Partridges; 9, Colombians; 12, Correspond; 13, Bemused; 14, Scratch; 15, Informally; 19, Desist; 20, Savage; 23, Muff; 24, Zero.

No. 58

Across: 1, Pivoting; 5, Aliens; 9, Mentally; 10, Adjoin; 12, Oleate; 13, Beverage; 15, Transmission; 18, Church-warden; 23, Bandanna; 24, Assisi; 26, Ocular; 27, Revision; 28, Stewed; 29, Hedgerow.

Down: 1, Pompom; 2, Vented; 3, Tractor; 4, Nell; 6, Ladders; 7, Egomania; 8, Singeing; 11, Denmark; 14, Knowing; 16, Scabious; 17, Burnouse; 19, Chamade; 20, Ensuing; 21, Tidier; 22, Winnow; 25, Mete.

No. 59

Across: 1, Understudy; 6, Scar; 9, Noyau; 10, Gangplank; 12, Kleptomaniacs; 14, Venetian; 15, Wyvern; 17, Renown; 19, Flea-pits; 21, Protectorates; 24, All Blacks; 25, Irate; 26, Ease; 27, Straighten.

Down: 1, Ulna; 2, Dry skin; 3, Roulette wheel; 4, Tightwad; 5, Denim; 7, Charade; 8, Rakishness; 11, Penny-farthing; 13, Every place; 16, Clarissa; 18, Noodles; 20, Instant; 22, Tacit; 23, Dean.

No. 60

Across: 1, Pompeii; 5, Waspish; 9, Non-stop; 10, Realist; 11, Character sketch; 12, Allice; 14, Robinson; 17, Departed; 18, Remain; 21, Photograph album; 24, Sincere; 25, Contain; 26, Tiddler; 27, Residue.

Down: 1, Panacea; 2, Many a slip; 3, Extra; 4, Impute; 5, Ward-room; 6, Shark bite; 7, Idiot; 8, Hitchin; 13, Corporeal; 15, Starboard; 16, Hear-hear; 17, Deposit; 19, Nominee; 20, Spacer; 22, Owned; 23, Agnes.